TURNING AROUND TURNAROUND SCHOOLS VOLUME 2

Embracing the Rhythm of the Learner Year

PRAISE FOR EMBRACING THE RHYTHM OF THE LEARNER YEAR

"In Frank DeSensi and Joe DeSensi's latest book, *Turning Around Turnaround Schools: Embracing the Rhythm of the Learner Year,* they introduce the idea of a yearlong story arc in which students journey through discrete stages (i.e., "sprints") in their development toward becoming strong, independent learners. Throughout the book, the authors remind us that true and lasting school improvement efforts place the learner at the epicenter of every decision. They debunk and replace conventional wisdom with brain research, conceptual learning theories, and practical information that any educator can follow. The recommendations and tools are applicable to all school systems, regardless of where they fall on a proficiency continuum. I highly recommend educators read this book to maximize student performance-based planning, create flow to the school year, and reap the assessment benefits that are sure to follow."

Ingrid L. Wiemer, PhD
Educational Leadership and Policy Studies - Loyola University; Retired Teacher, Principal, and Executive Director; Retired Adjunct University Instructor; 34 Years in Education

"To improve student learning, schools need strategies and tools. But because there's no shortage of strategies and tools in the school improvement marketplace, the challenge is to find the *right* ones. If you're looking to make significant improvement in student learning, look no further than this book to find a blueprint for improving learning for *all* students. Put the ideas from *Embracing the Rhythm of the Learner Year* into practice, then use the tools that support the ideas, and you *will* get results."

Bob Petit
Retired Educational Leader (Jacksonville, FL)

"When looking for a new, fresh way to attack turning around a school, I search for proven examples and suggestions that actually seem doable. Frank and Joe bring just that to administrators and educators in their second book, *Embracing the Rhythm of the Learner Year*. Thanks to their insightful concepts and a variety of checklist tools to help keep a school on track, change seems certain to happen. I am truly excited to share this resource with my colleagues and staff!"

Nicole Pacholski
Assistant Principal, St. Matthias School (Chicago, IL)

"During my years as a superintendent and principal, I was always looking for fresh ideas and frameworks for improving student outcomes and inspiring teachers. This book goes a long way toward doing exactly that."

Dr. Floyd E. Williams, Jr.
Chief Education Officer, HR Educational Complex

"I've been an elementary school teacher for the past five years and have come to think that it is time for meaningful change in K-12 education. My first school was a 'Turnaround School,' where a new administrator came in to raise scores, make sure students met standards, etc. We focused on 'old-school' methods, such as teaching-to-test. While test scores are important, we need a fresh new approach and outlook for teaching our students. *Embracing the Rhythm of the Learner Year* is a fresh new perspective on how to meet the needs of students in the classroom. I hope that other teachers will be inclined to read this detailed and informative text."

Jenni Weinstein
First-grade teacher, Tanaka Elementary School (Las Vegas, NV)

TURNING AROUND TURNAROUND SCHOOLS VOLUME 2

Embracing the Rhythm of the Learner Year

FRANK DESENSI | JOE DESENSI

SILVER TREE PUBLISHING

Turning Around Turnaround Schools, Volume 2:
Embracing the Rhythm of the Learner Year

Copyright 2020 by Frank DeSensi and Dr. Joe DeSensi

Published by Silver Tree Publishing, a division of
Silver Tree Communications, LLC (Kenosha, WI).
www.SilverTreePublishing.com

Editing by:
Jessica Gardner
Kate Colbert

Additional Editing by:
Susan Draus
Heather Tolle
Iam Bennett

Cover design by:
Lorenne Marketing & Design
Iam Bennett

Typesetting by:
Courtney Hudson

Comics and other graphics by:
Iam Bennett

First edition, April 2020

ISBN: 978-1-948238-30-4

Library of Congress Control Number: 2020901497

Created in the United States of America

DEDICATION

To our entire Educational Directions, LLC, ("Ed Directions") family, who made this book possible. This book is the remarkable outcome of the 20+ years of research and fieldwork that tested our ideas and ensured they worked in the real world. We thank you for your years of service in education, as well as your continued passion for innovating new research-based approaches to new educational challenges. We could not have written this book without every contributor, every sharp idea, and every bit of hard work across these past two decades.

TABLE OF CONTENTS

PROLOGUE

Embracing the Rhythm of the Learner Year is the book we have
wanted to write for more than a decade. In our two editions of the
first volume of *Turning Around Turnaround Schools*, entitled *What
to Do When Conventional Wisdom and Best Practice Aren't Enough*,
we needed to do a deep dive into our approach to education. This
second book — Volume 2 in the *Turning Around Turnaround Schools*
series — takes that educational framework and breaks it down into
student-focused, just-in-time sections of the school year. In some
ways, this is a radical re-envisioning of planning and learning based
on the neuroscience of student learning and performance. In other
ways, this is just a student-centric approach to education that has
a lot of good horse sense and practical applications.

> Breaking down the educational framework into
> student-focused, just-in-time sections of the school year
> is a radical re-envisioning of planning and learning based
> on the neuroscience of student learning and performance.
> It's also quite simple — a student-centric approach to
> education that has a lot of good horse sense and practical
> applications.

The origins of this "Rhythm of the Learner Year" process actually date
back about 25 to 30 years, with some specifics on how to open school

and close school in a bookended way that maximizes what those time periods can offer. As we began to fold in the emerging neuroscience research in terms of students putting things into and retrieving from long-term memory, the story arc of the *learning year* started to take shape. In the early 2000s, we first connected the flow of each unique segment of the school year and Summer Period to one large iterative cycle. A few years later, arguably the most critical piece of the puzzle — differentiating between the Formative and Calibrating Periods — took shape.

Since then, we have been sharpening the saw, as Stephen Covey would say. We continually refine these processes, add activities, and integrate the questions and clarifications back into the core processes and tools. This book covers the yearlong story arc of the just-in-time professional development (PD) sessions we offer to the school districts or specific schools we have been asked to help.

One of the reasons for writing this book is that it can take a couple of years to fully understand the entire process, and even those teachers and administrators who have participated in our professional development programs need a "manual" full of reminders and reinforcements. With the normal turnover and attrition that happens in administration and faculty, it became difficult to push deeper into the planning and strategies in the Rhythm of the Learner Year because we were on-boarding new staff each year. Also, with midyear changes in leadership or faculty, the new folks had a hard time catching up.

This book was written primarily for the people who would be attending our first year of professional development programs, but we have added some tools, processes, and checklists for those who might be entering year two of our PD cycle. This book is also intended to be a valuable resource to educators who have not collaborated with Ed Directions, but who are dedicated to embracing new philosophies and approaches for ensuring student success and school improvement.

We are proud to have helped turn around struggling schools and to have added value to blue-ribbon schools. This book is the aggregation of the research and fieldwork that has gone into our approach to working with both types of schools. We tried to write it in a step-by-step, show-your-math, chunked-out format so that if the leadership team at your school or district were never able to attend an Ed Directions PD program, they could still plan and monitor their school year with the student-focused understanding of the Rhythm of the Learner Year in mind.

INTRODUCTION

It was the same scenario over and over — every fall, teachers and students would start the school year optimistic and energetic. By the second week, teachers and students were frustrated with the fear that certain students were going to fail. Interventions were put in place, but, inevitably, the number of students expected to fail did. As long as student success was not tracked or linked to accountability, it was not seen as a major problem. Some students just *could not be taught.*

The accountability movement of the 1990s changed all that. Schools were suddenly required to make all students into "proficient" performers on state assessments and prepare all students to make more successful transitions into their next stage of education or their next stage of life in general. Each state developed education "standards" and standards-based assessments as part of this effort to hold schools accountable.

The progress data collected by the states highlighted schools that "consistently underperformed" and noted performance gaps between and among groups of students. State departments of education (DOEs) subsequently mandated that "unsuccessful" schools be "turned around." Accordingly, DOEs, district instructional leaders, and school leaders sought out remedies to turn things around. Millions and millions of dollars were spent on a variety of initiatives: different teaching strategies, new materials, new support systems, more teachers, fewer teachers, more technology, new leadership, etc.

School improvement plans got longer, referred to more data, and emphasized research. Most did not drastically improve student performance. Traditional learners continued to do well while non-traditional and at-risk students continued to underperform. Success stories existed but were the exception.

Success stories existed but were the exception.

Ed Directions was established in the late 1900s to support schools in their efforts to build "proficient" students and, if necessary, raise high stakes testing scores. In Kentucky, there is a popular saying about taking a trip. It goes something like this: "If you are going to take a trip, you need to know where you are, where you're going, and who's going with you before you make any plans." Our staff decided to use this trip-planning analogy to test school improvement plans.

We started with, "Do the schools know where they are?" We thought this would be the easiest piece to apply to the turnaround process because we had the test results. Like so many of our assumptions in those early years, we were not even close. Schools assumed that the state test scores represented an accurate gauge of student performance when, in fact, they didn't tell us about *why* students underperform, *where* their work broke down, or *what* was the root cause. At best, the fossilized data told us where the students were not. Schools built School Improvement Plans (SIPs) by using the previous year's scores as a starting point for setting priorities and goals for the upcoming year's planning.

The use of state or district test scores as a decision driver was problematic for several reasons:

1. The scores didn't tell us where the students were in terms of proficiency; they told us how many points they had earned on a paper and pencil test.

2. Without knowing more about why the students scored as they did (i.e., did they try and give their best effort, could they read the questions, had they been taught the critical concepts of the question, etc.), we couldn't tell with certainty where the school was last year.

3. Plans referred to last year's scores but had no data set on the current status.

After the first year, we found that not one of the schools we worked with collected any data on student performance as a learner or student performance on different types of tests. Not a single one. In terms of the Kentucky saying, they didn't know where they were.

Ed Directions' leadership decided that, upon entering the school, our first task was to get school leaders to understand that test scores are a *data* point (an important data point), but they are not a *decision* point.

The problem wasn't to turn around the adults in the building, to change staff, or to change curricular programs. The problem we had to deal with was turning around individual student performance in the school. Changing the school's focus on what drives planning helped us redefine the "where we are" and "where we are going" aspects of school planning. To do that, we had to attack traditional concepts of "best practices" and conventional wisdom about what makes a school a "good" school.

The issue of "Where are we going?" was also problematic. Most schools we worked with reviewed the standards and then chose the standard that matched what they were going to teach and referenced that standard in the lesson plans. "Backward planning" meant that teachers looked at the standard and then looked at where they taught the standard in their units and lessons.

We had to get schools to understand that the standards don't define what teachers must cover; they define what the students have to learn and what they have to do with what they learn. Standards defined expectations for student performance, not adult performance.

In addition, conventional wisdom held that "aligned" curricula and materials were the answer. Conventional wisdom was wrong. When we led curricula audits and referenced curricula to the standards learning set, we found that many of our schools were covering less than 25% of the learnings and competencies that could appear on the test. Until all teachers and students knew all that was expected from the state standards, planners had no real idea of where they were going.

In addition, conventional wisdom held that "aligned" curricula and materials were the answer. Conventional wisdom was wrong.

A big "aha" moment occurred when we did a flowchart analysis of the school improvement plans. Frequently, plans were developed using outdated data points and seemed to focus on changing the students who had been in school last year. We struggled to get schools to realize that the student cohort they had had last year had changed — they were older, they moved, new students came in, students forgot things over the summer, etc. Schools planning in this way was like driving by only looking in the review mirror.

Getting schools to deal with the "who" in *who had to change* was perhaps the biggest problem for school turnaround leaders. Conventional wisdom focused on changes in adults, but Ed Directions had determined that turnaround success depended on changes in students. In our study of school SIPs, we found that no school plan in our group dealt with plans to move students from where they were to where they had to be by test time. If schools wanted to develop intentional turnaround plans, they had to focus on moving the students that are in class this year and not the students that were in class last year.

Getting schools to deal with the "who" in *who had to change* was perhaps the biggest problem for school turnaround leaders. Conventional wisdom focused on changes in adults, but Ed Directions had determined that turnaround success depended on changes in students.

A corollary to the Kentucky travel adage was that you should check to see if you are getting where you want to go. In conventional wisdom, test scores were used to monitor progress. Our coaches had to get academic leaders at all levels to rethink data management and identify things like "point of break down" and root cause analysis of both learning work and assessment work.

This thinking led us to redefine all our work with schools and rethink "best practice." We had to get schools to focus on proficient learners and performers. They were accountable for test scores, so we had to improve scores on a paper and pencil test. However, to do that we had to focus on building student competencies. Higher test scores should be a byproduct of student performance-based planning, not the focus.

Higher test scores should be a byproduct of student performance-based planning, not the focus.

It became clear that if we wanted all students to be proficient by the time they took a test in May or transitioned over the summer to the next level, we had to develop an approach to intentionally provide students with work that would move them from where they were as learners and performers at the start of school to where they had to be by test time. Today, we begin all our school turnaround work with an examination of standards and what they mean, and then what the Rhythm of the Learner Year has to look like to enable all students to reach their potential as performers as defined by those standards.

THE RHYTHM OF THE LEARNER YEAR

In this book, we will emphasize both the neuroscience of how students learn and how they access that learning to perform at the level required when that learning is assessed/measured. We will look at the whole child, taking into account both cognitive and noncognitive abilities and indicators. This whole-child focus is the basis for the just-in-time approach to developing the culture and climate, unpacking standards, building independent learners, making those learners performers, winning hearts and minds to get the best effort for assessments, and mitigating the summer losses of content and process.

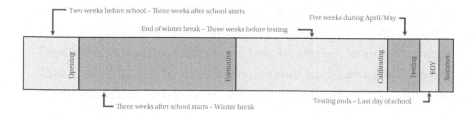

We split the year into discrete periods, each with priorities building toward an independent student learner and performer who understands proficiency and gives best effort. In the **Summer Period**, we evaluate data and plan for the year (culture and climate as well as teaching and learning).

In the **Opening of School Period**, we ensure operations are smooth, and the focus is upon building a learner-friendly culture and an optimal learning environment. In the fall's **Formative Period**, we build learners; we assess the root causes of those underperforming or off-grade and provide targeted support. In the **Calibrating Period,** after winter break, we focus on performance: the use of long-term memory in performing tasks at the level of rigor and complexity at which students have to work on the state assessment. As we approach the **Testing Period**, we have to open pathways back to that learning from the beginning of the year, make sure we have hearts and minds, and lock down the adult activities that are needed for a smooth testing cycle. We can consider the **End-of-Year Period** a chance to mentally pack things away for the summer and collect information about the year for summer planning, professional development, and identifying operational strengths and weaknesses.

WHAT TO EXPECT FROM THIS BOOK

In this book, we will break each period down into priorities, best practices, and, in some cases, week-to-week game plans. The data that's needed and the metrics used to track progress will evolve through each period of the school year, all based on student-focused planning and a commitment to teaching the whole child. Once one begins to think of the school year as discrete sprints that develop and enable learners, the lion's share of leadership's focus becomes student work, data management, and solving the *right* problems.

The authors of *Embracing the Rhythm of the Learner Year* intend to share the research and firsthand experience that led us to first define where the students were going and then develop an approach that would support all students getting to that point. One crucial element has been a change in focus from what the *teacher* is teaching to what the *student* is doing to become more proficient at learning and performing. This required that we rethink the academic year. We had to move from adult schedule priorities — grading periods, etc. — to a year that represented student developmental cycles and priorities. We call this approach the Rhythm of the Learner Year.

As you dig into the content of this book, it may be helpful for you to know what's in store. Here is a quick look at the book's key sections and chapters.

In the pages that follow, we focus on what's expected of students beyond just content, and we look at a developmental sequence that enables all students to be successful. We describe the Rhythm of the Learner Year in terms of "periods," where particular types of student work produce optimal benefits for learners.

Chapter 1 focuses on what is required for students to be proficient learners and performers. It introduces how educators develop the relationship between how students learn and what factors determine their level of performance. It helps us define where we're going and gives us a rubric for determining where we are in our journey.

Chapter 2 introduces the Rhythm of the Learner Year with a brief description of each period and the period-specific goals.

Chapter 3 covers the Summer Period as a planning and preparation time for adults and looks at opportunities for reaching out to students and preparing them for successful entry into school.

Chapter 4 introduces the opportunities and priorities of the Opening Period of the school year. It focuses on the importance of developing classroom cultures and climates and building basic academic skills that enable students to be successful.

Chapter 5 looks at the Formative Period, which can be a time of significant growth and student potential. It emphasizes the need for more than a content curriculum. This is a time of not just content growth but also growth as learner, growth as performer, and growth as thinker.

Chapter 6 explores the Calibrating Period, when the focus switches from just building student potential to actualizing that potential. It develops the idea of gradually calibrating the nature and quality of student work until students are working successfully at the level of the assessment.

Chapter 7 looks at the Testing Period and distinguishes between successfully administering a test and building a best-practice testing environment. It focuses on opportunities schools must utilize to maximize student performance and get best effort for the Testing Period.

Chapter 8 explores the opportunities of the End-of-Year Period, covering how to end school with the student in mind, and not just adult survival. It also focuses on student work that can reduce performance loss over the summer, continue to build the student as learner and performer, and expand student operational language.

Chapter 9 revisits the Summer Period with a focus on opportunities for self-assessment and planning, student development, and teacher development that would not have been possible in the first summer. It looks at what summer activities are available after the school has spent a year working with the Rhythm of the Learner Year.

Chapter 10 summarizes the Rhythm of the Learner Year and reviews the Ed Directions process of introducing the Learner Year to district and school staff.

TOOLS, CHECKLISTS, AND GRAPHICAL ORGANIZERS

To facilitate the implementation of the ideas in this book, each chapter includes at least one real-life example and includes a sampling of tools that relate to the issues discussed in the chapter. Some tools are informational and provide more in-depth support for ideas in the chapter. Others are examples of student work mentioned in the chapter, and others deal with data collection strategies and monitoring student growth as learner and performer.

We have provided a book that is intended to inform the casual reader about how students grow while also providing a template for school practitioners and turnaround leaders to build student-focused plans, units, lessons, and assessments. To find tools discussed in this book, as well as new tools and information, please visit the Ed Directions website at EdDirections.com/LearnerYear.

01

FOUNDATIONS FOR THE LEARNER YEAR

Before launching into the just-in-time, student-focused approach
called the Rhythm of the Learner Year (Learner Year), we need to
visit some of Ed Directions' foundational ideas about the current
state of education. Then, we need to examine how standards-based
education works, how high-stakes testing changed accountability,
the current adult-focus in school planning, and the neuroscience that
allows students to put things in long-term memory (learning) and
access long-term memory and perform rigorous tasks (performing).
The focus of this book is breaking the school year into discreet
segments with building students' capacity to learn and perform
driving scheduling, resource allocation, and planning.

RETHINKING STANDARDS-BASED EDUCATION

The standards-based school accountability movement that started
in the 1990s was supposed to change the way schools did business
(their approach to education). While it did change the vocabulary
of educators and the way schools were held accountable, it did not
generate the structural changes anticipated by the school reformers.

Students, teachers, and administrators continued to work in ways that fit their comfort zones. There was some token use of "backward planning," progress monitoring, standards-based lessons, and rigorous work. However, the expected seismic change didn't happen.

Ed Directions was developed to help schools that were struggling to improve student performance in general or to reduce the performance gap between successful and less successful students. In the course of developing our strategies and toolkits, we have created a "go-to" core of research that we use when we first go to a school to refocus the school's perception of what the turnaround task requires.

TEACHING TO THE STANDARDS

Our first step is to reframe instructional leaders' and teachers' perceptions of their task of increasing student performance and raising school scores. We focus on the nature of the standards and emphasize that the standards don't define what must be taught. The standards determine what students must learn and the level at which they must use what they've learned. Ed Directions will often conduct a curriculum audit to unpack the state's standards and then check the status of the school or district curriculum in terms of what those standards require.

Toolkit Item Available
Download at www.EdDirections.com

Ed Directions uses a proprietary process that we call *Unpacking a Standard*. Ed Directions' teams use it in a curriculum audit to begin the process of planning an intentional curriculum. This toolkit introduces the process of *unpacking a standard*, the complexity of the learning packages included in an English-Language Arts (ELA) standard, and the levels of rigor that all students at a specific grade level must reach before they take the state test. In a school setting, the "unpacking" tool can be used by administrators to track what is taught, what is learned, and what students can do with what they've learned as it relates to a specific standard. Academic leaders and instructional or content support staff can use it to help teachers develop intentional courses, units, and lessons — intentional in terms of what the students must learn, do with what they've learned, and the level at which they have to do it.

The reading standard shown on page 18 is an example of the learning package found in a typical state standard. In the first step of defining a standard, each standard is "unpacked" to identify its critical elements — essential vocabulary, expected tasks, and possible test formats. This process yields a list of learnings similar to those in the example.

Learning Breakout Overview – Critical Learnings of the Standard

Standard	Critical Vocabulary		Tasks	Possible Test Items
L.A. 5. RL. 1.	Explicit meaning	Reading strategy	Identify the main idea	Multiple-choice
	Literal meaning	Reading for information	Identify supporting details	Hot text selection
	Inference	Literature	Show supporting detail impact on the development of the reading	Identifying correct inference or conclusion
	Conclusion	Informal writing	Recognize and show how language is used	Multiple selects
	Text	Story	Drawn inference or conclusion and support	Drag and drop text into response
	Phrases	Excerpt	Use the text feature to facilitate unlocking meaning	Drag and drop text to support an inference or conclusion
	Sentences	Folktale		Extended response question
	Main idea	Legend		
	Key idea	Newspaper article		
	Central idea	Magazine article		
	Theme	Poem		
	Supporting details	Drama		
	Relevant details	Play		
	Language choice	Map/chart/graph		
	Audience	Inset/graphic		
	Purpose	Picture		
	Character	Inset		
	Emphatic/expressive language	Text features		

THE PROBLEM WITH VOCABULARY – UMBRELLA TERMS

The collection of learning includes concepts, relationships, and tasks that can be taught and used to create test items that are consistent with the standard expectations. However, many of the terms included in an unpacked standard represent a collection of learnings. These collective terms must themselves be "unpacked" to identify the complete standards expectations — vocabulary, tasks, etc. — that can appear on a state assessment.

In working to a standard, teachers must understand that stating the standard or providing work that fits under the standard umbrella is not sufficient to prepare all students to be proficient. Test writers *unpack* a standard and then select priority examples to build into test questions. If students haven't mastered the complete learning set for the standard, they can *know* what they've been taught but miss questions because their education didn't include either the specific learning required or adequate preparation in how to demonstrate their knowledge.

At Ed Directions, we refer to these collective terms as "umbrella terms." Examples of umbrella terms pulled from sample tests that reference the sample standard unpacked above include:

Learning Breakout – Text Features

Abstracts	Diagrams and plans	Bold or highlighted text	Captions	Change font size
Charts	Indexes	Epilogue	Footnotes	Glossaries
Headings	Lists	Insets	Introduction	Italics
Latin roots	Rubrics	Maps	Pictures	Prologue
Quotes		Support materials	Table of contents	Tables

For all students to be prepared to deal with text features, they not only have to master identifying the different types of features but must learn to use them to do what is required on the state assessment. For example, they may need to use text features to unlock meaning or use a text feature in conjunction with text to answer a question or make a decision.

At an elementary school, a large number of students missed a question asking why a particular word was in italics. The students had never seen the word "italics," and only those who were extremely independent thinkers were able to guess that the one printed in a different font was the one referenced in the question. Unless they guessed correctly, everyone else got the question wrong or skipped the question entirely. They were prepared to identify "text features" but not italics.

Dataset Item Available
Download at www.EdDirections.com

For another example, a social studies question presented students with a cartoon and a prompt that set the historical environment for the image. The question asked the students to identify the persuasive techniques the artist was using in the comic. In one of the schools where an Ed Directions coach was working with students, several students skipped the question. When asked why, the students explained they had never analyzed a cartoon and didn't know what persuasive techniques went with them. The problem wasn't with the students' knowledge of general concept of *persuasive techniques*. The problem was they didn't know how to use their expertise within the context of the test question.

Every standard includes three essential components:

- First, critical conceptual vocabulary that students have to know and understand.

- Second, task vocabulary that defines the type of work students must be able to perform with what they've learned.

- Finally, assessment vocabulary that identifies the critical language and expectations of the state assessments, along with a description of the venue, format, duration, and rigor of questions that are found on the state test.

With an "aligned" curriculum that allows teachers to pick and choose what they will teach under a standard, we can have a situation in which the teachers teach, and the students learn. However, when the test writers chose to focus on a different element of the standard, the students missed a question. The students learned but didn't learn what was tested. It will appear in the "analysis" of the scores that the teacher didn't teach, and the students didn't learn, but this will be a "false read." Students can learn and still fail to correctly answer questions if they haven't learned all the elements embedded in the assessment.

As teachers implement standards, they must understand that they can't teach the whole standard in one lesson, nor can they only reference the standard and teach bits and pieces of it. The classroom curriculum must address the expectations included in all parts of the standard — the languages, the tasks, and the critical levels of performance. The classroom curriculum should then be the map teachers follow to move all students from where they are to where the standard says they should be by the time of the assessment. Without this type of map, students who have extensive life experience with language can sometimes overcome incomplete preparation, while those with limited life experience with language cannot.

During a curriculum audit, the Ed Directions team identified the learning packages included in the state ELA standards. When the team examined the district curriculum, they found that much of the state package was included. However, when observing the implementation in the schools, the Ed Directions team found that no schools were actually implementing the district curriculum as designed. The teachers had several reasons — there was too much to cover, the materials referenced weren't there, they hadn't attended the training, etc. As a result, they picked and chose what they preferred to teach or what they thought would be most beneficial to students. The central office had not observed this difference between the designed curriculum and what was taught, and school support staff only reported that teachers were or were not following the daily pacing guide.

Today, Ed Directions emphasizes that instructional leaders must understand that in a world of high stakes accountability, academic leaders must attend to multiple curricula, including the:

- State assessment and transition expectations.
- District curriculum designs.
- School or grade level curriculum plans.
- Curriculum that is taught.
- Curriculum that is learned and used by all students.

Failure at any level of the curriculum can put districts, schools, and students at risk. It can also create or exacerbate underperformance by at-risk students and increase performance gaps between groups of students.

Once educators know what's in a standard, they need to understand what that implies for all students. State standards don't describe learning goals that some students will be able to master and others won't. They are standards of performance expected from all students. The standards describe what all students must learn, what they must be able to do with what they learn, and the level at which they must be able to do it.

Ed Directions considers standards to be minimum competencies expected of all students before they can be regarded as "successful." This means that academic leaders and teachers need to understand how students learn and why they perform at the levels at which they perform before they decide what is "best practice."

HOW STUDENTS LEARN

The standards require that students be proficient learners and proficient performers. They do not require that the teacher stays on a daily schedule, follows an established routine of lessons, or provides required whole-group remediation for struggling students. They do require that schools and teachers develop a curriculum that makes all students proficient learners and performers who can demonstrate their potential on a paper-and-pencil test or make a successful transition to the next grade level or the next stage of life.

Teachers and academic leaders must understand the "standards movement" changed the game. Before the standards expectations, school improvement focused on changing teaching strategies or the adult work in a classroom. Ed Directions coaches refer to this as planning on the "input" side. Usually, these plans include new teaching strategies, new programs and materials, new technologies, or new professional development for teachers. Teachers were evaluated on their implementation of the new strategies or the use of the new materials. Nobody checked the impact of the implementation on student learning and student performance.

It is critical in school reform efforts that everyone understand that standards proficiency requires more than just content coverage. Classrooms are missing a significant element needed in standards-based education if the teacher focuses only on:

- Making sure everything in a district curriculum is taught.

- Making sure that every lesson included in a district or state curriculum is delivered.

- Making sure that all students use every technology kit or strategy.

Today, many schools still try to turn around a school by only addressing around the adults in the building. They look for new lesson plan models or critical thinking skills they can implement as a part of teacher lessons. The problem for school reformers, however, is that the learning and the resulting use of learning at a level of rigor that is considered proficient is not a product of teacher work. It is a product of student work as a learner and performer.

The real job of the teacher is to prepare a map that enables students to do the work needed for them to be able to demonstrate their potential as a proficient performer. This involves identifying where the students need to be by the end of the lesson, unit, or course and then planning and engaging all students with a work sequence that will enable them to be learners and performers.

To understand the importance of this concept in the classroom, teachers must understand how students learn. The Ed Directions' approach was adapted from brain mapping research and the work of Robin Fogarty in how the brain learns. We emphasize the basic process of learning — attending work, acquiring work, organizing work, and meaningful work — that moves the students from an awareness level to independent proficient use of the learning.

In our model, learning begins when we become aware of a sensory stimulus, which is always present. The stimulus may be mental, physiological, emotional, or educational. Learners are often unaware of the stimuli and discard the learnings in milliseconds. This process is done in a part of the brain that some researchers call the sensory memory. It processes and discards or moves on information quickly.

For learning to take place, the learning must be *attended* (the learner has to be aware of its existence and its need to be learned), and the learner has to do something to *acquire* the learning. Without attending and acquiring work, there is no learning.

How Students Learn – Complete Model

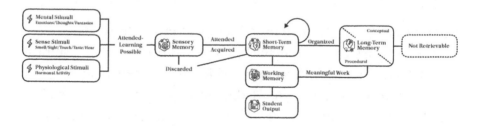

How Students Learn – Sensory Memory

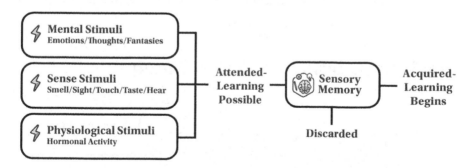

The importance of this phase of learning is recognized in early childhood education. Preschool and kindergarten classrooms focus on attending and acquiring as a part of their social and emotional development. They introduce rituals and routines that help students focus and engage in learning tasks. Almost every preschool, kindergarten, or first-grade class has some attention-getting/active listening ritual that students learn. After that, it disappears from the curriculum, but the need for expanding the students' attending and acquiring skills continues to grow through life.

Early in the school year, teachers need to focus on active listening, focused viewing, and critical reading as attending strategies that can support lifelong learning. Without developing these attending strategies, students will listen to and attend to things that interest them, are unique, or are unexpected. They will appear to be engaged, but in reality, they are not actively attending to the learnings of the lesson or activity.

Once students can attend to the things that must be learned, they must move the learning from the brain's sensory memory to a storage area called the short-term memory, which allows them to remember and to do work using their knowledge. This is called acquiring work. It is work that the students must do to begin taking ownership of the learning. A common example of acquiring work is notetaking. The students must take the notes. The teacher can model or teach strategy about notetaking, but the students must do the work. The teacher cannot work or learn for the student.

How Students Learn – Short-Term Memory

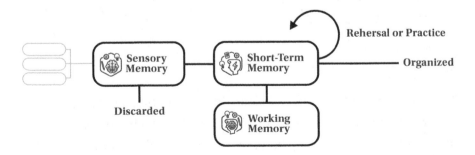

Early in the school year, teachers need to make sure students can attend and do acquiring work (e.g., effective notetaking, highlighting, paraphrasing, etc.). By the end of the third week of school, teachers should check to make sure that every student can attend and acquire all of the critical learnings that will be developed during the year. Without this competency set, there can be no real learning — especially not the deep or meaningful learning consistent with the state assessment.

In the first weeks of school, the professional learning community (PLC) discussions need to:

- Look at student attention, attending work, and acquiring work.
- Identify inadequate work product.
- Determine where the process broke down.

Determine why it broke down so that the student can receive immediate targeted assistance.

Once information is in their short-term memory, students can work with the learning. They can engage in discussions, complete worksheets, and participate in question-and-answer sessions. They can take and pass tests if tests are given in a relatively close timeframe to learning the information. The problem with short-term memory is that it only lasts from two days to a week. This is why students can acquire learning, participate in a review, and pass the test, but later, remember neither the learning nor the test.

Recent research indicates that by third grade, many students are short-term memory dependent. They assume that they must remember something for the unit test, and they prepare as if the learning set of the unit is relevant only to that test. Many of the students will do well in end of unit tests, but they will not do well on cumulative tests such as a state proficiency test or any other test used to measure collective academic development.

For students to build lifelong learnings, they have to move their learnings from the short-term memory to another storage area called the long-term memory. Some research indicates that long-term memory lasts a lifetime, and if we can get information stored and cued in long-term memory, it will be available for an end-of-the-year assessment.

How Students Learn – Long-Term Memory

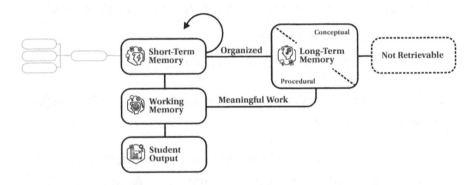

Educators face several problems in building working long-term memory:

- There are many types of long-term memory: emotional memory, episode memory, personal memory, etc. For example, many students — especially younger students — tie their learnings to the teacher. When the teacher is present, they remember their learnings. When the teacher is not present, they don't.

- Only two long-term memories are tested: the conceptual memory where we store concepts, relationships, visuals, etc., and the procedural memory where we remember how to perform tasks or procedures that were part of the learning set.

- Getting information stored in long-term memory is not the only issue. The information must be independently usable in real-world or assessment situations that are not tied directly to the class. This requires that students do some work with the learning that creates meaning for that learning. Teachers can't create meaning for students, but they can provide work that will help students construct meaning. Meaningful work usually involves the student's use of learning in a thinking activity or a real-world application.

If we get students to attend, acquire, organize, and create meaning, we have created effective learners. When the goal is that all students will be successful, this learning sequence (or one like it) must be the core of every curriculum. If educators want students to be successful learners, they must teach to "successful learning" as well as deliver content.

Another piece of conventional wisdom that can be problematic is the assumption made by teachers and, unfortunately, by state assessment scores that if a student misses a question, that student did not know the content. This is more "wisdom" that has to be discarded. Effective learners may or may not be effective performers. Teachers must understand that delivering content and building proficient learners is only a part of their task. Unfortunately, students can learn effectively and still perform poorly on assessments.

WHY DO STUDENTS PERFORM AS THEY DO – THE 5 LEGGED MODEL

Ed Directions emphasizes that several factors determine the level at which students will perform. When we started researching this idea, we initially identified three factors that determined how students perform as they do. Today, we emphasize five legs that support performance. The importance of this part of our work can't be underemphasized. Many students know the material but fail on tests because of factors other than knowledge of content.

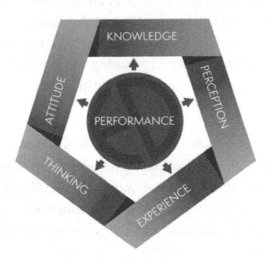

The 5 Legged Model emphasizes that students must have a knowledge base. If they don't know the content or if they haven't learned to perform specific tasks or procedures, they can't be proficient on an assessment that requires knowledge of content tasks. Learning is critical but not sufficient. For a student to demonstrate their full potential on a test, five areas of competency must be developed:

1. The first leg is ***Knowledge.*** State assessments establish expectations for all students. Each student must own the learnings (concepts, tasks, thinking) required to meet these expectations. This critical vocabulary needs to be operational, not just known. Without an adequate knowledge base, proficient performance is not possible. It is necessary but not sufficient for proficiency on high-level tasks.

2. The second leg, *Attitude,* relates to the student's willingness to invest self in learning and performing. If the student knows the content but will not give their best effort on the test, the student will not be able to represent what they know fully. For students to demonstrate their potential as performers, they must give their best effort, stay engaged, and complete all tasks. To a great extent, their attitude defines their willingness to do this.

3. The third leg is *Perception*, which is closely tied to attitude. Many perceptions are included in state standards (e.g., perception of time, perception of distance, etc.). Two perceptions that are not included in state standards but are critical to student performance are *perceptions of proficiency* and *self.*

   a. *Perception of Proficiency*: Because assessments are written to a defined level of rigor and complexity, they require students to understand that this is what proficiency requires and how to work to that level. Unfortunately, many students don't understand what proficient work looks like or what level of engagement and effort proficient work takes. Many students finish the task and are satisfied that they have met the expectations. Others assume that if they did any work, that it is sufficient. If students do not have a perception of proficiency and proficient work, they can know the content and still perform poorly on a rigorous test.

   b. *Perception of Self*: For a student to demonstrate his or her potential on a cumulative assessment, the student has to have a level of competence and confidence that encourages them to believe that they can be successful. Perception of self will determine whether students can accept academic challenges, work out of their comfort zone, or take on complex tasks — all of which will be required on high-level cumulative assessments.

Both perceptions are often linked to attitude, and one can cause change in the other. Students with low self-esteem frequently develop bad attitudes about classes where they don't feel they can be successful. Likewise, students who are adversarial in their relationship to adults or who have authority issues can develop perceptions of self that do not include their best effort.

Much of the work done with attitude and perception indicates that these are developed early in life. One study demonstrates that analysis of attitude and perception in first-graders could identify the students who would not become good readers or would not be proficient in math. Another study of third-graders led the researchers to determine that they could predict with some degree of accuracy who would fail algebra, who would fail English, and who would drop out of high school before finishing their senior year.

4. The fourth leg is *Thinking (or metacognition)*. Building a learner and performer requires building a thinking base that includes habits of the mind (e.g., seeking clarity, identifying requirements of the question, overcoming impulsive responses in generating thoughtful responses, etc.). It also involves thinking strategies like decision-making and problem-solving. Successful learners and performers think about *how* they have to think. They think *about* and they think *with* content and create extended meaning for the content. State assessments presume thoughtful habits of mind and require critical and creative thinking to get maximum credit on complex questions.

5. The fifth leg is **Experience**. Becoming a proficient learner and performer requires an experience base that builds the knowledge, skills, habits of mind, and thinking strategies needed for learning and performing. For students to perform successfully at

the level of their potential on a rigorous, complex test, there are two sets of experiences that are critical:

a. Teachers have to understand the knowledge base represents the "taught" curriculum. It is developed through student work that is designed to enable deep learning of content, tasks, skills, strategies, and methods. The other four legs aren't taught. They are formed and shaped as students work and think about content. They are developed by the "experienced curriculum" but have to be intentionally included and developed as teachers plan units and lessons.

b. Additionally, teachers must understand the need for successful equivalent experience (work that is consistent in rigor and duration). For students to predictably work at the level of difficulty included in a test, almost all require successful experiences working at that level before they take the test. Very few students can develop a comfort zone around a low level of rigor in their work and then jump successfully to a higher level required on a test. If their prior experience doesn't prepare them with a comfort zone that embraces the level of difficulty and complexity of a test, they are not ready for the test.

Teachers must develop a curriculum map that addresses experience. The experience set must escalate student learning work and assessment work until students reach the level required to exhibit proficiency on a test. While most curricula try to be intentional about the "taught" curriculum, they allow the "experienced" curriculum to develop in an accidental and nonsequential pattern that is usually unsuccessful in moving all students.

Classwork, which provides the bulk of the students' experience with learning and performing, can have a positive or negative effect on students. Successful experience builds a comfort zone of success, fluency, competence, confidence, positive attitudes, and positive perceptions. Inappropriate work or unsuccessful experience creates a comfort zone that accepts failure. It undermines confidence, builds negative attitudes and perceptions, and does little to prepare students to extend themselves on assessments.

A principal at one of our schools questioned whether this was as important as we tried to make it. To test it, she picked a young girl who seemed to be a struggling writer. She then worked with her Ed Directions coach to address the student's perception of self as a writer by building escalating and cumulative successes from building a great sentence to building a strong personal narrative. The principal worked with the student for less than a month before the assessment, working only on attitude and perception. On the test, the student moved from a novice writer to a distinguished writer. The principal did not teach writing ... she changed the student's perception of writing and of self as writer.

A principal at one of our schools questioned whether this was as important as we tried to make it. To test it, she picked a young girl who seemed to be a struggling writer. She then worked with her Ed Directions coach to address the student's perception of self as a writer by building escalating and cumulative successes from building a great sentence to building a strong personal narrative. The principal worked with the student for less than a month before the assessment, working only on attitude and perception. On the test, the student moved from a novice writer to a distinguished writer. The principal did not teach writing ... she changed the student's perception of writing and of self as writer.

When we begin work in a school, the 5 Legged Model is presented to staff, and they are asked how they would develop each of the five legs. In most cases, the staff develops a list of random activities that relate to one of the five legs, but the randomness of the activities undermines the effectiveness of those activities in developing the necessary competencies. If we take the "developing the whole child" research seriously, we can identify numerous reasons why schools embrace the 5 Legged Model:

- Students come to school performing at different levels because of differences in ability and differences in life experience. The more experience students have with language and language development before they come to school, the further they will be ahead of students who lack language experience. Building the five legs that support proficiency in all students helps erase a part of the gap, while failure to develop the five legs can increase the performance gap between students.

- Difficulties with any of the five legs can cause students to perform below their potential. Difficulties in more than one leg can cause students to perform well below their potential. Teachers have to accept that students can know the content but perform as if they didn't know the it because of attitude, perception, thinking, or experience issues.

- The five legs of the model don't just support student performance on tests. They support student work as learner, thinker, and real-world user of learning.

For all students to become proficient, they must have intentional curricula that support the development of all five legs. There must be a taught curriculum that is congruent to the standard expectations in language, task, format, rigor, and thinking and an experienced curriculum that builds the five legs that support performance.

CHAPTER 1 APPENDIX – TOOLS

There can be many umbrella terms under the same standard. In this same standard, different genres are mentioned. Analysis of test items identified several genres that can serve as a venue for reading questions.

Reading: Expected Genre Experience

- Children's stories or fairytales
- Rhymes
- Short stories
- Plays

- Novels
- Scripts
- Journals
- Magazines
- Newspapers
- Brochures

- Non-fiction
- Speeches
- Editorials
- Advertise-ments
- Schedules

- Recipes
- Forms
- Atlases
- Instructions
- Memoirs
- Cartoons

- Legends
- Poems
- Graphic novels or stories
- Manuals

In the summer before school opens, teachers need to assess the genre expectations for their grade level or their subject matter and determine if it is taught, where it is taught, and at what point do we expect students to master the use of that genre.

Genre Summary – Self-Assessment

Genre	Taught Where?	Students Mastered Where?

The Proficient Student – Expected Characteristics

Characteristic	If present, the student ...	If missing, the student ...
Regular and prompt attendance	If present on time, the student has the opportunity to learn and share equally in learning experiences.	The student can't learn if not present and can't get equal experiences if tardy.
Active, engaged listening	The student who listens actively has the opportunity to acquire the critical learnings and directions delivered verbally.	Lack of active engagement means a student will miss much of the learning set presented verbally.
Independent learning	Identifies required learning and seeks to acquire; "learns to learn."	Depends on the teacher to identify what must be learned and provide the work that leads to learning.
Attention or engagement control	Can control attention and engagement as required by the task; "alert and engaged."	Is impulsive, loses concentration, and fails to maintain engagement.
Prioritizes critical learnings	Can separate "needs to know" from "nice to know" from simply interesting information. Understands what has to be learned and what's to be done with a learning.	Remembers those things attended and not important. Will frequently link learnings to the teacher or to a story and not to the critical meaning or details.
Can work independently from long-term memory	Independently works from long-term memory. Links task to prior learnings.	May need teacher support to do best work and may have a pattern of working from short-term memory.

Characteristic	If present, the student ...	If missing, the student ...
Communicates using critical content vocabulary	Can separate "needs-to-know" from "nice-to-know." Owns the critical language required for a task.	May "know" but be put off by the language of the task. May communicate in informal register effectively but struggle when formal is tested.
Understands operational vocabulary and plans complete responses	Uses the critical vocabulary required by a task (e.g., knowledge, oral, written vocabularies).	Is unable to "unlock" the requirements of the task. May "know" but be unable to "use."
Format mastery	Has mastered the format(s) included in an assessment. Knows how to engage each type of task (e.g., computer testing).	May have to do additional thinking, have confidence problems, or miss questions because of format issues, not lack of knowledge.
Critical reading	Utilizes appropriate strategies (purpose, genre) for the task. Applies logic and reason to reading.	May be a good "recreational" reader but unable to do the thoughtful reading required by a test. May give impulsive or illogical responses to thoughtful questions.
Varies reading rate according to purpose	Understands critical reading requires more attention to meaning in detail than recreational reading and chooses the reading rate appropriate to task.	Many students are recreational readers and have one reading rate that does not allow the critical examination of text required on state assessments.
Critical thinking	Effectively uses independent and critical reasoning and thinking skills required by a task.	May rely of impulsive, rote, or ritual responses instead of thoughtful, reasoned responses.

Characteristic	If present, the student ...	If missing, the student ...
Critical writing	Writes to the task requirement. Communicates in writing as required by a task. Produces reasoned and logical writing.	May rely on impulsive or ritual writing. Has difficulty translating thinking into text.
Engagement experience	Has worked successfully at the levels of engagement required by a task or assessment.	May have a "comfort zone" unequal to the task. Can "know" but must work at a lower level than the assessment.
Appropriate attitudes	Engages tasks willingly and with appropriate effort. Gives "best effort" on every question.	May be unable to give consistent "best effort." May not be able to "endure" long tasks.
Perception of proficiency	Knows what proficient work looks like and what it takes to produce it. Believes he/she can work at that level.	May believe work at required level is "impossible." May produce work assumed to be proficient when it is not.
Self-evaluation and revision to proficiency	Independently examines work produced and judges match to task requirements. Revises as needed.	May seek completion not proficiency. May make but not correct errors. May expect any work completed and submitted to be acceptable.
Completes assigned tasks, self-checks, and revises	Acquiring an understanding of what's required by a task and following the work required through to completion is a significant strength of the proficient student.	Failure to seek clarification of what's required or failure to complete the required work is the mark of an immature learner and causes students to perform below their potential on assessments.

Characteristic	If present, the student ...	If missing, the student ...
Completes homework and prepares for class	Preparing for class and completing homework are part of the learner work pattern associated with proficient students. This ensures the students engage in work that is appropriate learning work.	Students who fail to complete homework are not prepared for class and miss out on activities that are beneficial not only for learning but for developing learning habits leading to lifelong learning.
Extends learnings beyond the classroom	Proficient students see applications of schoolwork in the real world and seek to learn from experiences beyond the classroom.	Students who exhibit very little curiosity or initiative relative to the relationship of what they're learning to the real world are frequently unable to act in situations that are not traditional classroom situations.
Participates in co-curricular and extra-curricular activities	Participation in co-curricular and extra-curricular activities encourages different types of learning and provides opportunities for leadership.	Students who don't take advantage of activities outside the classroom frequently see school as an intrusion and become alienated from the learning process.
Participates in and serves as leader in academic and nonacademic activity	Most proficient students have multiple opportunities to be leaders in academic and extracurricular activities. This enables building of brain patterns and leadership qualities essential for success in the real world.	Students who never seek or were never allowed to participate in leadership activities miss a critical set of learning experiences that relates to brain development, social maturation, and emotional maturation.

The Proficient Student – Growth Sequence

Characteristic	End of Grade 2	End of Grades 3 and 5	End of Grade 8
Regular and prompt attendance	Begins to take responsibility for getting to school.	Takes responsibility for getting ready for school and getting to school on time.	Accepts responsibility for getting ready for school and getting to school on time.
Active, engaged listening	Pays attention when addressed and follows instructions.	Engages in active listening, seeks clarity, and provides feedback when appropriate.	Is an active critical listener who seeks clarity and detail and provides both short-term and long-term feedback.
Independent learning	Works independently with a peer group and learning situations.	Can work independently as learner and performer but may need teacher prompt or monitoring support.	Can learn by working independently, in small groups, or in whole class situations. Takes responsibility for learning.
Attention or engagement control	Can control attention for at least five minutes and stay engaged in tasks for the same length of time.	Can stay attentive or engaged for at least 15 minutes and refocus if pulled off task.	Can stay attentive or engaged for at least 30 minutes and can refocus if pulled off task. Can control the level of engagement based on the complexity of the task.

Characteristic	End of Grade 2	End of Grades 3 and 5	End of Grade 8
Can work independently from long-term memory	Is beginning to work from long-term memory but may still be teacher-dependent to pull content knowledge from long-term memory.	Can work independent of the teacher if the work is in the student's comfort zone. At the end of grades 3 and 5, student must be able to work from long-term memory and at the level consistent with the assessment.	Can work without teacher presence or teacher prompt to access long-term memory and use learning in high-level, complex tasks.
Communicates using critical content vocabulary	Can communicate with the initial critical vocabulary of reading and math.	Can communicate with discipline-specific language, if prompted, but prefers informal register. The formal register will be required on the test.	All school-related communication involves content-appropriate vocabulary in formal register.
Understands operational vocabulary and plans complete responses	Can understand tasks and follow thinking processes through at least three steps.	Understands that tasks and operations require specific steps in planning and has strategies for determining what's required for proficiency and then working to that level.	Unpacks directions, identifies tasks needed for completion in the rubric for proficiency, and plans a proficient response.

Characteristic	End of Grade 2	End of Grades 3 and 5	End of Grade 8
Format mastery	Has mastered short response, multiple choice, and initial electronic assessment formats.	Has mastered short response, open response, electronic, multiple choice, and other assessment types as found on the state assessment.	Has mastered short response, open response, electronic, multiple choice, and other assessment types as found on the state assessment.
Critical reading	Is primarily a recreational reader but should have a perception of reading to learn and reading to respond.	Emerges as a critical or strategic reader who understands how to read to perform a task.	Reads critically and purposefully to learn or acquire data for problem-solving and decision-making.
Varies reading rate according to purpose	Exhibits grade-level speed in recreational reading.	Reads critically at a rate consistent with the expectations of the state assessments.	Reads critically at a rate consistent with the expectations of the state assessments.
Critical thinking	Can solve simple problems and follow one-, two-, or three-step thinking problems. Can learn to respond in a Statement, Reason, Evidence (SRE) pattern.	Can solve problems, make decisions, and draw conclusions requiring up to five thinking steps and can respond orally or in writing in an SRE pattern.	Can solve problems, make decisions, and draw conclusions requiring up to seven thinking steps and can respond orally or in writing in an SRE pattern.

Characteristic	End of Grade 2	End of Grades 3 and 5	End of Grade 8
Critical writing	Can explain a thought or solution and provide a reason and evidence.	Can communicate thinking, decisions, or solutions to a problem clearly and in a logical order.	Can communicate thinking, decisions, solutions, or reactions to data clearly, using appropriate vocabulary and logic.
Engagement experience	Can identify work that they have done successfully that is at the level of the assessment.	Identifies assessment level work and determines if the work he or she produced is proficient.	Identifies assessment level work, determines proficiency, and revises to proficiency, if needed.
Appropriate attitudes	Understands best effort and can give best effort to learning work and assessment work.	Gives best effort in learning and assessment work. Accepts challenges and takes academic risks.	Accepts difficult challenges, takes academic risks, and seeks personal best. Frequently identifies alternative or tangential applications.
Perception of proficiency	Understands what grade-level proficient work looks like and how to produce it.	Identifies his or her work as proficient, identifies what's wrong if it is not proficient, and corrects the work.	Understands proficiency and seeks to produce proficient work. Seeks support or assistance to increase the level of performance.

Characteristic	End of Grade 2	End of Grades 3 and 5	End of Grade 8
Self-evaluation and revision to proficiency	Regularly checks work to make sure it is correct, and revises work if prompted.	Checks work without teacher prompt and revises to proficiency. Seeks support, if needed.	Independently checks work, identifies flaws, and refines product to proficiency. Seeks instruction or direction, if needed.
Completes tasks assigned in class	Follows most reading and math work through to conclusion.	Completes school tasks in a timely fashion with a focus on completing all parts of the task.	Completes school tasks and reviews work to ensure all parts of a task are completed proficiently.
Completes homework and prepares for class	Requires parental assistance but completes homework in class preparation.	Understands the purpose of homework and links homework to class learning. Looks ahead to the next day's lesson to prepare materials.	Links homework to learning and to the next day's work, completes the homework, and gets the materials needed for the next class together.

Characteristic	End of Grade 2	End of Grades 3 and 5	End of Grade 8
Extend learnings beyond the classroom	Makes initial links between what's learned in school and the real world.	Is curious about the world outside the classroom and recognizes some learnings in the real world. Is able to link learning to a real-world scenario found on an assessment, if prepared to do so.	Is able to engage in discussions about the application of learning in real-world situations and produce multiple real-world examples of specific learnings. Can identify real-world applications and respond or explain orally or in writing what the application is.
Participates in co-curricular and extra-curricular activities	Shows enthusiasm for opportunities for interest activities. Art, music, and problem-solving build brain patterns and benefit other subject areas.	Can follow an interest independently and seek improved performance through practice. Mastery of any area will impact brain function, confidence, and attitude.	Is capable of very high-level engagement in extracurricular and co-curricular activities. Superior performance increases confidence, changes in brain activity, attitude, and perception of self.
Participates in and serves as leader in academic and nonacademic activity	Alpha students tend to assume most leadership opportunities unless students are intentionally engaged in leadership opportunities.	Since leadership experience builds attitude, self-perception, and problem-solving ability, all students should have some experience with leadership.	All students need multiple opportunities to serve in a leadership position. Leadership experience is a significant variable in building independent responders and performers.

THE 5 LEGGED MODEL QUICK REFERENCE

Knowledge: State assessments establish expectations for all students. Each student must own the learnings (concepts, tasks, thinking) required to meet these expectations. This critical vocabulary needs to be operational, not just known.

Attitude: Students must know the learning required. Additionally, they must be willing to perform the necessary tasks and invest a "best-effort" on every part of the assessment. Every answer or product should represent the student's personal best effort.

Perception: Most state assessments embed perceptions generated by learning. There are two perceptions required for student performance that are not related to standards expectations:

- **Perception of Proficiency:** The student knows what constitutes good work and how to produce it.

- **Perception of Efficacy:** The student believes, "I can work successfully at the levels required."

Thinking: Mature thinking patterns and critical reading and writing are required on every question of a state test.

Experience: Almost all students need two sets of experiences: they must have work experience that forms the five legs, and they must have experience working successfully at the level of the assessment. In other words, they must have both formative and calibrating experiences.

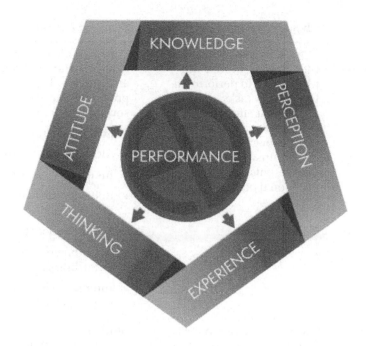

	Why It Is Important	**Problem Causes**
Leg 1: **Knowledge**	State assessments establish expectations for all students. To meet these expectations, each student must own the learnings (concepts, tasks, thinking) required. This vocabulary must not only be known but must be operational.	If critical learnings are not known or are not operational, students cannot perform the required tasks. This knowledge base must be congruent with the task for students to reach their potential. Alternative languages and level experiences can produce a gap between potential and performance.

	Why It Is Important	**Problem Causes**
Leg 2: Attitude	Students must know the learnings required and be willing to perform the necessary tasks, investing their best effort on every part of the assessment. The expectation is that every answer or product represents the student's personal best effort.	Poor attitude usually causes a student to learn and perform below potential. It leads to several problems: • Low motivation. • Attention problems. • Inefficient use of time. • Behavior or socialization issues. • Loss of concentration. • Attendance problems or tardiness. • Intentionally not giving their best effort.
Leg 3: Perceptions	Most state assessments embed perceptions (time, space, distance, etc.). Two perceptions required but not related to standards expectations are: • Perception of proficiency: Knowing what constitutes good work and how to produce it. • Perception of efficacy: The belief, "I can work successfully at the level required." Students must know what good work is and believe they can produce it, or they will not demonstrate their full potential.	Students operate in a comfort zone built by experience as a learner. If a student believes shoddy work or inadequate effort is good enough, he or she will work at that level on any assessment. If the student believes she or he cannot do the work required, she or he will be correct. Lack of belief in self produces anxiety and can negatively impact attitude.

	Why It Is Important	**Problem Causes**
Leg 4: Thinking	Mature thinking patterns and critical reading, writing, and thinking are required on every question of a state test.	Immature thinkers, impulsive responders, and attention-deficit students regularly misread questions, leave tasks unfinished, and produce products that lack depth and integrity.
Leg 5: Experience	Almost all students need two sets of experiences. They must have work experience that forms the five supporting legs, and they must have experience working successfully at the level of the assessment. They must have formative and calibrating experiences, where differentiation and accommodation become critical.	If the student lacks the appropriate experience, she or he can know the content but be unprepared to work at the required levels.

02

THE RHYTHM OF THE LEARNER YEAR

It took several years of research along with trial and error working with schools for us to develop an approach for focusing school decision-making on *student* needs instead of adult or curricular needs. This research and implementation experience caused us to rethink how educators need to do business in schools. It also caused us to rethink what we considered educational "best practice."

Most of our staff were administrators or educational coaches and were comfortable with the body of *conventional wisdom* that they had used in their schools and districts. It became apparent we had been making decisions that were inconsistent with the task of developing proficient learners and performers. This made us uncomfortable. When we self-analyzed how we designed systems and curricula, we identified several issues that were inconsistent with what our research said we should be doing. The issues included:

- Most management systems were designed to accommodate adult responsibilities and accountability.
- Most educational systems were designed around an academic year divided into adult-mandated reporting and grading periods.

- Many school and classroom rituals and routines were designed to make the adults' jobs easier.

- The focus on courses, units, and lesson planning was to make sure content was covered (but not necessarily learned).

- Assessments were designed to provide a basis for giving students a grade (and not for guiding student learning).

After a particularly trying year working with turnaround schools, our leadership team decided to look at what we had to do with students and then think about how we had to redesign schools to make those changes in students.

We approached the research on how students learn and the five legs that support their performance. We looked at what had to happen to make sure that both of those models (i.e., *How Students Learn* and the *5 Legged Model*) were developed in every student. In discussing attitude and perception, for example, the research indicated that it was difficult to change attitude and perception unless the culture and climate of the school and classroom were *explicitly designed* to provide experiences that changed attitude and perception.

We had addressed culture issues before, but we addressed them when we had a chance to work with staff on the elements of culture. We found that the later in the year we waited, the more difficult it was to change the culture and thus to change attitude and perception. We needed to rethink how to start school with the climate and culture that students need to build positive attitudes and perceptions.

Similarly, in discussions around how students learn, we found that schools and teachers rarely included work that built learner proficiencies. We assumed that students would learn or not learn, and if they didn't learn, we would remediate them. We came to understand that if we wanted to build proficient performers, we had to first build proficient learners and then enable them to use what they learned on a complex task.

Toolkit Item Available
Download at www.EdDirections.com

We decided that we needed to redesign the school year around the learner needs and, for the time being, ignore the adult divisions of semesters and grading periods. At first, we identified three periods: the opening of school, the first semester, and the second semester, but this model did not provide us with enough time and structure to implement plans for all students.

Eventually, our model evolved into a year-long cycle of planning and implementation — all focused on student needs — the Rhythm of the Learner Year. In this model, the student year begins in the summer and moves through five distinct periods before the next summer cycle begins:

- **The Summer Period**: The Learner Year starts with the Summer Period. Adults examine the expectations of students and assess the students they'll have to move toward those expectations. We emphasize that in summer, the focus is on getting the school and the staff ready for the students that teachers will have in class the upcoming year.

- **The Opening Period**: Schools must understand that the Opening Period is critical. Ed Directions coaches say you can't win the school year in the opening weeks, but you can sometimes lose it. It's that important. The focus of the Opening Period is to get the students ready for the school. It is a time to equip them with the things they need to be successful and to develop the rituals and routines that will enable them to do the learner and performer work that they will need to grow toward proficiency. We like to say that if we have students who do not behave, cannot do the work required, or have not mastered critical rituals and routines, we haven't opened school. In several of the schools in which we worked, the staff was still trying to open the school as a learning institution in December or even March.

- **The Formative Period**: If we have equipped students for success, our task becomes to make them more proficient learners and build their potential as independent performers. The focus is on building proficiency doing all the levels of learner work in developing the five legs that will support proficient performance in the next period. The Formative Period is critical. We can achieve a year's growth of student potential in the Formative Period if we get all students highly engaged in rigorous learning work.

- **The Calibrating Period**: If we have managed to get students to develop as learners, we must add a new task. If students can learn, we have to prepare them to demonstrate what they have learned on a complex, rigorous test of long-term memory. The learning experiences started in the Formative Period continue, but students must also engage in escalating experiences (experiences that become more rigorous and complex), equivalent experiences (experiences working at the level of the state assessment), and calibrating experiences that gradually increase the rigor and complexity of both learning work and assessing work.

- **The Testing Period**: Another example of a period that is critical but not in itself sufficient is the Testing Period. Most schools seek to administer tests in an efficient manner that is consistent with state confidentiality and ethical requirements. The distribution of time, the organization of students, and other decisions are driven by an adult need to have an efficient, trouble-free testing cycle. There is another way. If we look at the Testing Period from the student perspective and focus on building an optimal assessment environment, we have to deal with a different set of priorities. We found there are things we can do that make taking tests less stressful and more manageable from the students' point of view and create an optimal environment for students.

- **The End-of-Year ("EOY") Period:** The End-of-Year is often overlooked as administrators and teachers seek to get everyone out of the building successfully and without suffering casualties. In this push, schools often miss an opportunity to deal with student performance issues (e.g., performance loss over the summer, loss of work ethic, etc.) by failing to provide effective cumulative or capstone work. The EOY is critical for organizing long-term memory, linking common learnings across disciplines, and preparing for successful grade transitions.

Our work with the Learner Year turned out to be very beneficial in our turnaround program. We needed to set goals that focused on where the students needed to be and then accept that we had to design the Learner Year to get them all there. Only then could we convince teachers and school leaders to look at changing their school's "way of doing business" without casting blame or immediately talking about students' deficiencies. It enabled us to be proactive in a nonthreatening way.

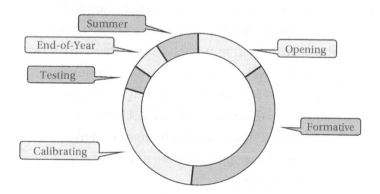

When Ed Directions works with a school for the first time, the leadership coaches try to get the school academic leaders and the teachers to attend a brief introduction to what we mean by *student work* and then use that introduction to build student experiences for the Opening Period. This almost always reduced the number of students expected to fail and created a more positive classroom culture.

The success rate of students in this approach encouraged all staff to continue planning the culture and climate, building courses, units, and lessons that were more intentional about moving every student. There was less concern about covering all the content and teaching all of the lessons included in the district guide and more of a focus on building competent learners and performers. When the teachers combined this approach of planning student work with the development of academic and behavioral rituals and routines that emphasized optimal learning conditions, they found that the culture and climate of their classes changed noticeably, and the level of student growth improved significantly.

In debriefing with schools after we started working with them on the Learner Year, we found that teachers were very upbeat about their work. Teachers reported feeling not threatened by this approach (as they may have been previously when the central office introduced a new program or material set) and that they could use it to help make classroom work relevant for the students. Many said that developing the Learner Year approach caused them to set up their classrooms differently, select materials more intentionally, change the focus and nature of PLC discussions, and build support and remediation programs that provided support beyond mere content review. They concluded that dealing with learner needs throughout the Learner Year made them much more intentional in their planning and their teaching work.

One teacher said the most valuable thing that she learned from her work with Ed Directions was to write the test first and then design the student work to make sure that all students could learn enough to pass the test. She said this changed the way she developed her lessons (around student work) and the way she provided support.

One teacher said the most valuable thing that she learned from her work with Ed Directions was to write the test first and then design the student work to make sure that all students could learn enough to pass the test. She said this changed the way she developed her lessons (around student work) and the way she provided support.

Several data points support the idea that the Rhythm of the Learner Year is a viable approach to both turnaround schools and successful schools that want to increase student potential (and as a byproduct, have higher test scores). These points include:

- Rather than punishing off-task behaviors, most schools that use this approach of building and standardizing behavioral management rituals and routines that establish optimal learning behaviors, positively changed classroom behavior and climate and reduced referrals and suspensions. In one school, the result was astounding. Their serious infractions and suspensions were reduced by 90 percent in the first semester.

- Many students decide in the first week or two of school whether they will pass a subject. If they believe they won't pass at the end of the third week of school, they probably won't. In schools that build effective academic rituals and routines, most found that they could reduce the number of students who felt they had no chance to pass to zero.

- Teachers found that focusing on equipping students with strategies for success in the Opening Period and by building learning competencies in the fall, they increased the rate of student content coverage and the amount of content retained in a usable, retrievable fashion in long-term memory.

- Data management over the Learner Year allows for immediate reaction to a specific condition that reduces student performance. Support and remediation systems can be targeted to groups for students who have the same priority need and not just the same score. Reaction time to a learning and performance problem is reduced significantly, and students get targeted assistance, not blanket assistance.

Sometimes nonacademic issues complicate the process. High teacher and student absences can render the sequence of work ineffective. Additionally, any number of other problems (e.g., bus schedules, substitute availability, delayed material arrival, etc.) can make it difficult for teachers to develop an intentional sequence of work. If school staff fail to build a "user-friendly" learning environment, increasing numbers of students will perform below their potential.

CHAPTER 2 APPENDIX – TOOLS

RHYTHM OF THE LEARNER YEAR – AT A GLANCE

We use **the Rhythm of the Learner Year** for:

- Building independent, proficient performers.

- Building a comfort zone around best effort.

- Establishing an accurate perception of "proficient" learning and performing.

- Prioritizing effective engagement in critical reading, writing, and thinking strategies in content work and assessment.

- Building compensating and accommodating strategies where performing competencies are lacking.

- Providing only effective learning and performing work in all classes.

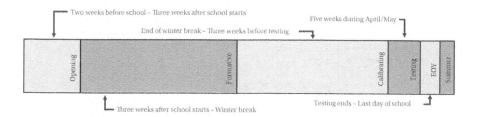

STEPS FOR REDESIGNING LEARNERS

- Establishing learning and performance goals.

- Planning for optimal learning.

- Differentiating for learning and performance.

- Implementing best practice(s).

- Monitoring and adjusting the plan.
- Providing multiple learning opportunities.
- Providing targeted interventions.

THE RHYTHM OF THE LEARNER YEAR PERIODS

- Summer Period
- Opening of School Period
- Formative Period
- Calibrating Period
- Testing Period
- End-of-Year Period

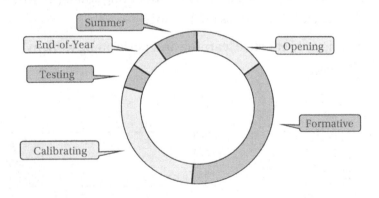

THE SUMMER PERIOD

Timeframe: From the end of school to two weeks before the start of the next year.

Priorities:

1. Reducing performance loss.

2. Encouraging interests and talents.

3. Building access.

4. Reviewing of data.

5. Planning, planning, planning.

THE OPENING OF SCHOOL PERIOD

Timeframe: Two weeks before school opens to three weeks after school opens.

Priorities:

1. Enculturation.

2. Preparing all students for success in class.

3. Mastering management, academic rituals, and routines.

4. Building adult access to students.

5. Establishing work and performance expectations.

6. Jump starting critical reading, thinking, and writing.

THE FORMATIVE PERIOD

Timeframe: From week three to the beginning of winter break.

Priorities:

1. Building an independent learner and increasing potential as performer.

2. Building operational language.

3. Using critical reading, writing, and thinking strategies.

4. Building basic reading and performing competencies.

5. Building a best effort comfort zone.

THE CALIBRATING PERIOD

Timeframe: From the end of winter break to three weeks before the state test.

Priorities:

1. Building proficient performance.

2. Mastering uses of content.

3. Successful equivalent performance.

4. Operational language fluency.

THE TESTING PERIOD

Timeframe: Up to three weeks before the test, the testing cycle, and the week after the test.

Priorities:

1. Enabling long-term memory.

2. Ensuring best effort.

3. Transitioning to the EOY work.

THE END-OF-YEAR PERIOD

Timeframe: Two weeks after testing ends until the last day of school.

Priorities:

1. Establishing student ownership of learning and performing.

2. Enabling successful transitions.

3. Establishing summer expectations.

03

THE SUMMER PERIOD

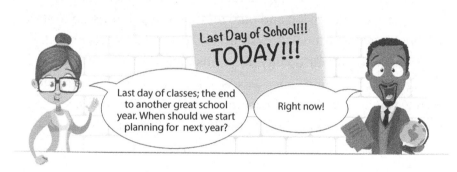

Description: The Summer Period is a time for evaluation, planning, and preparing. If treated as a part of the Learner Year, it can be a time of growth and expansion for students and teachers. For the administrators, summer is a time to determine what went right last year and what we need to do better during the upcoming year. In the second half of the summer, school academic leaders need to be engaged in strategic planning and preparation of facilities, programs, materials, and staff for the arrival of the students.

Timeframe: The Summer Period is divided into two sub-periods. The first sub-period (first half of summer) is devoted to an analysis of what did and didn't work in the previous year. This period begins with the end of the school year and lasts three to four weeks into the summer.

The second sub-period (the second half of summer) focuses on preparing the facilities and staff for the students who are going to show up on the first day of school. This period begins when the evaluation of the previous year is completed and lasts until the Opening of School Period begins — about three weeks before the students arrive.

Goals: In the first Summer Period of implementing the Rhythm of the Learner Year, the focus is on establishing a knowledge base and building a vision for academic leaders. Our coaches facilitate the development of the vision and plan for marketing that vision to staff and enabling the vision with systems and procedures. It is probably not possible to provide quality programs for teachers and students during the first summer since access to teachers and students will not have been planned and may not be available. For the first year, the goals for the summer tend to focus on academic leaders. These goals include:

- Develop a vision and strategic plan that can be turned into tactical plans by all staff.
- Sort and place students to create effective teaching and learning teams.
- Get the facilities, materials, and technologies in efficient working order.
- Evaluate and upgrade management and academic systems.
- Provide the ad hoc PD needed to prepare staff to lead learners and learning teams.

Leadership Priorities:

- Complete a self-assessment of the previous year's successes and failures.

- Establish an academic leadership team.

- With the team, develop a vision of a successful, student-focused school.

- Develop a plan for marketing the vision to staff and, eventually, students and their parents.

- Assess school systems — management and academic — to ensure that they are consistent with and will support the new vision.

- Assess staff preparation and identify ad hoc professional development that will be needed for teachers and support staff to implement division.

- Assess the curriculum and materials to make sure that they are consistent with the vision.

- Develop a strategic plan (which can be the SIP) for rolling out the new direction and monitoring its implementation and impact on students.

- Developing a preliminary student profile set to identify students who will start the year "at-risk" or who need special assistance to start the year successfully.

Readiness for Summer Work – Self-Assessment

Best Practice Indicators	Yes/No	Priority
Did we reach the goals we set in our SIP? Do we know why or why not?		
Do we have a plan for evaluating what worked and what didn't work this year?		
Have we evaluated all of our academic and management systems and developed plans for changing those that were not "best practice?"		
Have we identified our staff for next year, and do we know what PD they need to be successful?		
Have we developed a student-focused SIP for next year?		

Often, our coaches are asked to work with a group after the opening of school, and we miss the opportunity to get leadership engaged in student-focused planning and systems revision. When this happens, the coaches are forced to develop ad hoc plans to create an awareness level and a set of fundamental understandings that they can use to get the staff started in building student-focused classrooms.

When it is possible to work with academic leaders before the teachers and students arrive, the coaches prioritize their goals based on the needs they identify from school and district data and conversations with the school leaders.

In the best-case scenario, the coaches could begin working with the staff at the end of the previous school year to facilitate an evaluation of what worked and what didn't, who worked and who didn't. Then they would move on to introduce the leadership team to the Rhythm of the Learner Year and the leadership opportunities that are available to them in the first year of planning around the Learner Year.

In the first year, a significant initiative is preparing the school and the academic leadership staff to develop and support effective teacher/learner/performer teams. The adult work and development over the summer is critical, but not sufficient, to make all students effective learners and performers. What it can do, however, is begin the process and start building the foundation. We decided it would probably take more than one year to get teachers to the practitioner level and would require ongoing ad hoc PD through the first and maybe the second year. A surprise conclusion that we reached was that it might take students one to two years to develop the habits of mind and the work ethic that they need to have to be effective learners during the Learner Year. This caused the coaches to begin looking for "student PD" in the areas of developmental learning work — "learning to learn" — and directed learning, thinking, and performing formative work.

We concluded that the coaches' and academic leaders' accomplishments in the first summer would be limited by the time left between the decision to employ the Rhythm of the Learner Year and the opening of school, and by the extent of compliance work that the district expected from school leaders in the second half of the summer. Some of the things that can be developed include:

- An abbreviated assessment of the previous year.
- Awareness-level PD for school academic leadership (and ideally district academic leadership).
- Practitioner-level PD and facilitated planning for academic leaders.
- Facilitated systems analysis.
- A facilitated analysis of available student data to identify students who are "at-risk" based upon attendance, prior academic or testing problems, or behavior patterns.

THE EOY SELF-ASSESSMENT

Those of us who were school administrators talk about the end of school with a sigh of relief and a feeling of gratitude that we ended the year without any major disasters. We now agree that this was probably not the best practice, but it took us some time to agree on what would be the best way to begin the summer.

During the first summer, there probably won't be time to do a full evaluation of the previous year, so it will be necessary to do an abbreviated version. This will include an evaluation of the school goal in terms of assessment scores, transition statistics, and speculation as to what happened if we didn't reach our goals. If possible, the Ed Directions coaches try to include an analysis of last year's school improvement plan (SIP). Goals, objectives, and target scores are identified and then compared to the school status at the end of the year and to this year's scores, if they are available. This type of self-assessment gives the school an organized approach to see if they finished where they intended. Any missed goal, objective, or target becomes the subject of a "data dive" to help leadership staff to identify how far off actual practice was from the goals set and develop a speculative menu of possible causes.

In this initial self-assessment stage, multiple reasons may be identified as possible causes of underperformance and missed goals. Sorting the menu into possible adult causes and possible student causes establishes a foundation for moving the leadership team toward a new type of student-focused planning that moves beyond scores and labels.

One school set a very aggressive reading goal and scored significantly below expectations. The immediate assumption was that the reading program did not work, and the school needed to look for a new approach to reading. A data dive, however, showed that only one reading teacher or coach who started the year at the school finished the year at the school. At one grade level, five different teachers and six substitute teachers worked with one of the classes before the test. Additionally, the school went without a reading coach until December and didn't get all the materials required for their reading program until January. The data dive didn't solve their problem but indicated that there were several possible causes for underperformance other than the nature of the program itself.

This is why the root cause analysis is essential. Assuming a cause and fixing the wrong problem is not an effective strategic plan. Students didn't perform poorly in reading because they didn't have a reading coach or because they didn't have teachers. They performed poorly because they didn't know or couldn't do something they were required to know or do. Once we know what the root cause was — why they couldn't do it — we can identify the impact of the other conditions and evaluate whether the reading program could have addressed the root causes if implemented effectively. Without the root cause analysis, we "guess and hope" instead of "analyze and plan."

As a follow-up, our coaches use a systems analysis checklist to evaluate their planning process. In most cases, the state or district dictates the planning templates schools are required to use that frequently don't address all the elements of a best-practice strategic plan. Using a best-practice checklist to evaluate last year's plan can be a vital first step in getting schools to realize that they have to pre-plan *how* they're going to plan to achieve the results that they want.

Ed Directions' tools for an end-of-year analysis and a planning process analysis are included in the toolkit linked to this chapter. The Ed Directions coaches use them to transition into planning for this year, but school leadership can use them to focus on successes and concerns from last year as a stimulus to faculty input on planning. Teachers can use the planning evaluation sheet to make sure that grade level and discipline plans are intentional, implemented, monitored, and evaluated for impact.

THE INITIAL ACADEMIC LEADER PD

During the first summer's planning, it is vital to identify the leadership team's preparation for academic leadership (curricula and learning) as well as managerial leadership (operations, facilities, busses, etc.). Since many leadership certification programs focus on managerial issues and legal and financial expertise, Ed Directions tries to plan an introductory workshop to establish baseline understandings of learning and the Rhythm of the Learner Year to act as a "call to action" for academic leadership.

In some cases, this workshop starts with an assessment of the leaders' professional development experience to-date, but in all cases, the workshop addresses:

- What standards-based education requires.
- How students learn to the level required by the standards.
- What factors determine the level at which students will perform.
- Using our knowledge of the students who will be in school this year and what do we know about them (initial student profiles).
- Expectation-based data management.
- Designing courses and units to reflect student proficiency.

- What teachers need to know about student work and designing lessons around student work.

DEVELOPING STUDENT PROFILES

One point emphasized in the leadership workshop is the opportunity to develop preliminary profiles for all the students using the data that's available from district and school records:

- Lack of academic success.

- Discipline issues.

- Attendance.

- Prior test underperformance.

- Identified physical or intellectual limiting conditions.

These preliminary profiles can identify students who have had very little academic success, who are behind their cohort group, who have attendance or tardiness problems, who have behavior issues, or who have special needs (physical or cognitive). Having this information in-hand can help teachers develop preliminary support plans for students who have known "at-risk" patterns and determine what specific learning and behavioral rituals and routines might be designed to support students' development of learning competencies. It can help if academic leaders can distribute students into classrooms where they can be effective learners and avoid creating toxic teacher/student mixes. Ed Directions uses a template to identify cognitive and non-cognitive indicators to establish a preliminary learner profile on each student.

This is a check-for-understanding activity that moves from an adult-focused planning to a student-focused plan. In this step, the Ed Directions coaches ask the leadership team to review the decisions they made for next year's PD, curriculum and materials, and the schedule to see if the issues that showed up in the profiles are addressed. In most cases, they find that the decisions made represented central office dictates or adult preferences and didn't relate to specific, identifiable needs of students. The selection of materials, the schedules, the support systems, curricular and extracurricular activities, etc. were all probably selected based on adult preferences or adult perceptions of what was best for students. In transitioning away from adult-focused planning to student-focused planning (changing the SIP from *school* improvement plan to *student* improvement plan), we try to focus academic leadership staff on expected outcomes before they talk about the input side of teaching and learning. This requires that schools look at a different set of data.

A simple version of an initial student profile is included in the toolkit links to this chapter. Some of the positive and concerning characteristics can be pulled from school records, while others can be filled out by prior teachers or by current teachers in the first weeks of school. Both administrators and individual teachers can use this tool to get both a whole-school perspective and a "my class" perspective.

DEVELOPING TEACHER PROFILES

A parallel emphasis in the leadership workshop is the opportunity to develop preliminary profiles for all instructional and support staff. Much of this information is available from district and school records and evaluations of performance done in the current and previous years. Some of the elements considered include:

- Teacher attendance.
- Teacher classroom control and discipline referrals.
- The performance of the teacher's students on district and state tests.
- Teacher rapport with students.

- Teacher involvement in co-curricular and extracurricular activities.

- Teacher success in leadership positions.

- Specific types or groups of students that are at-risk in the teacher's classes.

Comparing the teacher profiles to identified student needs provides data that can inform teacher professional development plans and intentional student/teacher placement.

The expansion of student and teacher dataset requires that academic leaders review their data management systems, identify data streams that inform decisions and data streams that need to be generated to inform decisions that will have to be made in the future. Some school systems have high tech options for aggregating disparate data sets. Some have data silos where some of this processing can be a manual process or rely on Excel or Access whizzes to collect the meaningful data needed.

DATA MANAGEMENT

Another element of the workshop is the redesign of the school data management plan. Changing school data management can be problematic. Most states and districts have data management technology systems in place that dictate the types of data that can be stored and retrieved. Also, most districts have monitoring assessments that are given and evaluated at the district level and even dictate the types of data that will be stored and used. For Ed Directions' purposes, these data streams can be used. They don't, however, provide some of the data points needed for teachers to make informed decisions about their students — especially about their students' growth as learner and performer.

One of the PD sessions in the Ed Directions leadership workshop deals with the development of a data room where the "compliance data" from state and district silos can be stored along with samples of student work as learner, student work as performer, work done in response to specific interventions or strategies, and data that relates to the impact of plans on student involvement in the teaching/learning process (e.g., attendance, optimal behaviors, etc.). The focus of the data room is to monitor the work students do as learners so that learner competencies can be developed that will enable all students to be successful. Another focus of the data room is to monitor student performance and identify the point of breakdown and the cause of breakdown so that intentional support programs can be developed.

In one school, a preliminary look at a critical non-cognitive descriptor — attendance — showed that every student who scored in the lowest quartile missed more than 15 days of school. No student who scored at the top-level missed more than five days. Further research indicated that this same pattern held for the past three years, but that the school had no attendance improvement plan in any SIP.

At the same school, analysis of teacher attendance proved to be equally significant. The average number of teachers absent on a given day was 11.5 (there were 26 teachers in the school). The lowest number of teacher absences was the first day of school when two teachers were absent. The highest number missing in a day was 18, and there were 17 absent on the day the science test was given. The average number of subs provided by the district was three per day. Concern for teacher absence was not identified as a priority of the school improvement plan even though unfilled absent teachers disrupted teaching and learning school wide.

Another data stream that becomes important when school opens is teacher effectiveness data. In the first summer, academic leadership needs to do a realistic assessment of teacher effectiveness. During this first year, some characteristics are critical to student success. These characteristics need to be monitored, and teachers need to be supported if they struggle. The initial assessment should include:

- Curriculum (course, unit, and lesson plans) development.

- Knowledge of content.

- Developing lessons that include best-practice student work.

- Planning for student proficiency.

- Generating and maintaining high-level student engagement.

- Development of optimal learning and performing behaviors.

- Data management.

- Differentiating learning and performing work.

- Identifying causes and providing shaping work and supportive assistance.

- Increasing student proficiency as a learner.

- Increasing student proficiency as a performer.

In reviewing this year's staff, if any teachers have identified weaknesses in any of these areas, support needs to start before the students arrive. Teacher competence in these areas is so important that good plans can fail, and students can fail to reach their potential, because a teacher or a set of teachers lacked critical competencies. Monitoring teacher effectiveness and supporting struggling teachers is a crucial activity for academic leaders and must be planned for teachers to come back to school.

The Ed Directions toolkit includes several templates for organizing cognitive and non-cognitive "risk" factors. A sample toolkit for dealing with non-cognitive characteristics that put a student "at-risk" toolkit is included in the appendix. It can be used by school leadership to identify schoolwide problems and develop schoolwide policies, procedures, and support systems. It can also be used by individual teachers to identify students in their classes who need immediate contact, encouragement, and support.

PREPARING TEACHERS FOR PLANNING STUDENT GROWTH

Most districts have policies and procedures in place that dictate how courses, units, and lessons have to be planned and delivered. This can be problematic if they are driven by content or adult decisions and not by student readiness and student need. Many times, the Ed Directions coaches identify student needs that indicate teaching and learning work outside the expected curriculum plan. These ad hoc considerations are sometimes prohibited by district policy, leadership expectations, or lesson planning models. In such cases, the coaches develop effective plans inside of the compliance plans.

One factor that's very difficult to overcome in a school is teacher buy-in. It isn't easy to get teachers to plan lessons around effective work based on current student status. Most schools teach lesson planning around content, teacher work, or specific materials. In several situations, teachers have balked about committing time or planning to learning goals or performing goals when they are evaluated on whether they are on the correct page of the district curriculum or if their students are reading the right story at the right time. Some teachers are evaluated to see if they are giving the required monitoring assessments on schedule (whether the students are ready for it or not.)

In preparing to start the year, teachers need to understand that, in a standards-based world, they don't plan to implement the district curriculum or the purchased curriculum. Teachers must plan to move the students from where they are to where they're expected to be by the end of a lesson, unit, or course. That becomes the curriculum map for that class. If teachers don't know what effective learning and performing work look like and don't know what building standards-defined competency means, academic leaders must provide appropriate ad hoc professional development and facilitated planning. This will enable teachers to plan to build learners and performers and not merely deliver content or stay on par with the curriculum guide.

The Ed Directions coaches use a number of evaluation tools they call systems analyses. The systems check for behavior management policies, curriculum, and culture/climate is included in the toolkit. The Ed Directions coaches use these tools to begin the school's self-assessment process and begin intentional, strategic planning. Academic leaders and teachers usually use these tools in the first summer to see if current practice is consistent with what standards-based expectations require in terms of behavior, curriculum, and culture.

ASSESSING FACILITIES AND MANAGEMENT SYSTEMS

The final stage of the summer workshop self-assessment is also a pivot into action planning for this school year. In this stage, the staff looks at students they have been assigned, what standards require, and compares all of their academic and non-academic systems against those expectations. Management and operations systems (e.g., bus patterns, operational management, grade reporting, staffing, etc.) must work efficiently and in the best interest of students. Ed Directions has found that management systems frequently determine what academic systems, programs, and strategies can be used in the classroom, and how or when they can be used. Purchasing procedures used in some states and districts can be out-of-sync with student need. When materials arrive in December and teachers are trained in their use in January, the program cannot be used as designed that school year.

The Ed Directions coaches use two tools to begin the discussion with academic leaders about school readiness for school to open. The facilities checklist provides school leaders with a list of facilities issues that relate to academic preparedness and safety considerations. Ed Directions' coaches use this with academic leaders to walk through the building, the classrooms, and the grounds to make sure that when students arrive, they will find a safe and organized facility ready for them to begin their learning work.

In one district, Ed Directions' coaches in several schools noticed that each school had a population of students that were performing well below the level of their peers. They designed an after-school and Saturday support program to target the priority needs of the students and help them close the gap with their peers. However, the district would not approve the plan because it would interfere with the bus schedule, and it would be too difficult to change the current busing plan.

Academic systems should also be analyzed as early as possible in the Summer Period. Many schools design curriculum and select materials without looking at the students they're going to have in the fall. Sometimes schools don't even look at the standards to see what is required of students before they make serious decisions about what will happen to students in class.

Looking at academic systems (e.g., behavior management rituals and routines, academic rituals and routines, progress monitoring, and data management, etc.) also involves a comparison to what's expected of students and what skills and deficits the students bring into the classroom. Reviewing the academic systems and comparing them to best practice doesn't have to be threatening for staff. It can be perceived as proactive — an activity to show us where we are going — and not as reactive or punitive.

In a school that had a score drop significantly, the Ed Directions coach was brought in after school started to help the school. His initial discussions with the school indicated they had no idea why their scores dropped. The principal made sure that every teacher followed the district curriculum and was always within two days of the pacing the district recommended. When the coach visited classrooms and talked to students, he found that most students couldn't do the work or work at the pace that was recommended by the district. In addition, very few students owned the operational vocabulary that was embedded in the activities and worksheets that supported the curriculum.

Almost every student in the school was confident that they were going to fail the year, and given their results on the work and assessments that had been given, they were probably correct. The coach's solution was to restart the very first lesson by doing a task analysis of the lesson and then teaching the students all the skills they would need to perform proficiently on the lesson's activities. They repeated this for every lesson in the two units that had already been taught. When the students were prepared for success, two things happened. First, they were successful at doing the learning work and on the assessments, and second, they no longer believed that they had to fail for the year. The coach came back to an Ed Directions meeting with a new saying for the company — "You can't start them where they aren't. You have to figure out where they are and start there."

> Reviewing the academic systems and comparing them to best practice doesn't have to be threatening for staff. It can be perceived as proactive — an activity to show us where we are going — and not as reactive or punitive.

The last activity of the leadership workshop is the development of a plan for opening school. For our leadership coaches, a primary goal is to *market* to staff a vision of a successful opening of school and then prepare staff to actualize that vision. Staff must focus on opening school with strategies in place to enable *all* students to be successful (knowing what success means, having access to support, and highly engaged and effective attending and acquiring work). It also means staff must spend time fine-tuning all systems — management and academic. Nothing good happens when systems fail during the opening of school. Facilities, technologies, and materials (both teacher and student) need to be ready for use. Data management, co-curricular, and extracurricular activities need to be designed, staffed, and scheduled. The goal is to make sure the school is ready for the students' arrival.

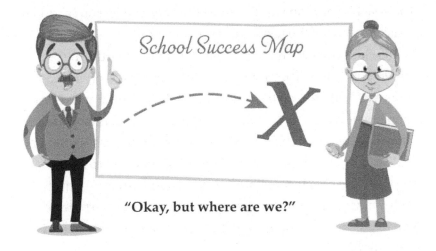

"Okay, but where are we?"

If we have access to the teachers before school starts, we encourage them to unpack the state standards for their grade level, review the list of the students they're going to have, and assess their own readiness to move those students from where they are to where they need to be. If there's any doubt that the teacher is ready to teach the students they are going to have in class and enable them to improve as learners and performers, the teachers and school leaders need to arrange for ongoing professional development, coaching, and support. This is a preliminary step for designing ad hoc PD for both the leadership team and the instructional and support staff. In Ed Directions' schools, all trainings end with personal action plans that define how the training will impact the participants' work in office or classroom.

If successfully marketed, this preparation work should lead to the development of an opening-of-school plan for every class that emphasizes preparing the students in that class for success. Part of this includes the design of diagnostic activities that can help teachers identify student strengths and weaknesses and establish a starting point for the teaching and learning activities that are going to move all students to proficiency. We emphasize that if the school wants to make sure it is ready for the students, it must quickly determine where the students are and update all plans for the first three weeks of school to reflect the learning needs of students.

Most Ed Directions' coaches find this means additional professional development to help teachers identify factors related to student success. In other words, factors that must be in place from day one for all students to understand what "success" means and what they have to do to be successful. It also means teachers may need facilitated planning to develop academic and optimal behavior rituals and routines. The first lessons must emphasize students doing attending and acquiring work so they can at least attend and acquire before they start the Formative Period.

It's important to remember that one of the initial goals for the summer was to get the school and staff ready for students' arrival. In best practice, this involves three things:

1. Data study and self-assessment to identify the academic goals for the year.

2. Assessment of staff's ability to meet the needs of the students who will be attending school when it opens.

3. All management and academic systems are operating efficiently and are sufficient to meet the needs of the students.

Ed Directions' coaches emphasize that the summer planning activities should enable schools — leaders, teachers, and students — to come to school prepared to have a successful year. Real learning cannot take place until teachers and students are ready for success and believe they can be successful. One of our coaches explained this to teachers who were struggling with attendance and discipline in December. When they asked him what was going on, he noted that it was December, and they still hadn't managed to open a school where teachers could teach, and learners could learn. Backing up and focusing on culture and the academic climate was critical to this school making progress that year. You can't move a school until you have properly opened it.

The final task for academic leaders is to make sure that the school — facilities, programs, materials and texts, staffing and staff, and critical student information — is ready for the students to enter the building.

SUMMER WORK BY GROUP – YEAR ONE

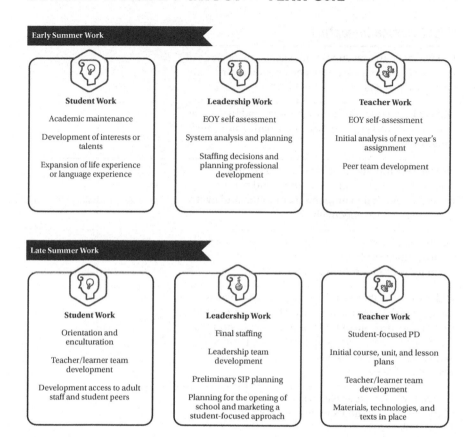

Early Summer Work

Student Work	Leadership Work	Teacher Work
Academic maintenance	EOY self assessment	EOY self-assessment
Development of interests or talents	System analysis and planning	Initial analysis of next year's assignment
Expansion of life experience or language experience	Staffing decisions and planning professional development	Peer team development

Late Summer Work

Student Work	Leadership Work	Teacher Work
Orientation and enculturation	Final staffing	Student-focused PD
Teacher/learner team development	Leadership team development	Initial course, unit, and lesson plans
Development access to adult staff and student peers	Preliminary SIP planning	Teacher/learner team development
	Planning for the opening of school and marketing a student-focused approach	Materials, technologies, and texts in place

By the end of the Summer Period, the school should be ready for students — facilities, grounds, systems, teacher preparation, etc. Teachers and administrators must have a plan for what activities students need during the Opening Period to ensure they enter the Formative Period believing they can be successful and owning the basic learning skills needed to do effective formative learning work.

Evaluating the Summer Period

Best Practice Indicators	Yes/No	Priority
Did we evaluate our success in each of the periods of the Learner Year and use that evaluation to drive this year's SIP process?		
Did we have staff and student profiles and use those to help staff and students select formative summer programs?		
Did we provide the summer programs that we selected with the financial, human, and material resources needed to implement, monitor, and evaluate the program effectively?		
Did the leadership team secure the experience and professional development experiences needed for them to be more proficient in their role?		
Did we formulate a vision of what the school was going to be like during the next school year, market that vision to all stakeholders, and provide support for stakeholders to develop the skills and understandings they need to be proficient in their role responsibilities?		
Do we have the expertise on staff to implement all of the priority elements within the SIP, action, and tactical plans?		
Do we have data that will demonstrate that our summer program had a positive impact on student competencies, teacher preparation, and planning?		
Have we evaluated our summer data and developed a menu of ideas for improving the summer experience for all stakeholders during the next Summer Period?		
Did we provide orienting and enculturating programs for new staff and incoming parents and students?		
Do we have a plan in place for ongoing orientation and enculturating for new teachers and new students?		

CHAPTER 3 APPENDIX – TOOLS

School Systems Review Toolkits

Culture Indicators

Self-Evaluation	Self-Assessment (1-10)	Priority (1–5)
Our school culture was designed with "best practice" in mind.		
All teachers believe all students can achieve the goals set by the state standards.		
The opening and closing of schools are designed to set the culture for one year and transition to the next.		
Rituals provide for all students to enter/leave on a positive note.		
Rituals are designed to be proactive, not reactive.		
Role group interactions are defined, modeled, and practiced.		
Inter- and intra-group interactions are monitored and shaped to exclude counterproductive interactions.		
The school is safe and welcoming. Students want to come to school.		
Diversity in style, rate, capacity, and processing is accommodated.		
All students get a chance to "produce" in their preferred mode (and enjoy success).		

Culture Indicators

Self-Evaluation	Self-Assessment (1-10)	Priority (1–5)
Parents are welcomed and are aware of access opportunities.		
Access issues have been analyzed, and all students have an "access route."		
Students have daily access to a teacher who can teach them.		
Classes are designed to build capacity in all students (to the standard).		
Classrooms are flexible and have resources for all students.		
Students have the opportunity for immersion, extension, and hands-on experiences.		
Students have the opportunity to speak informally to Administration.		

Planning System

Self-Evaluation	Self-Assessment (1–10)	Priority (1–5)
Our school's planning was designed with "best practice" in mind.		
The school's planning process is inclusive. All role groups are provided with access and encouraged to participate. **(Inclusive)**		
Planning is student-focused and driven by the school's success in moving all students to expected levels of performance. **(Student Focused)**		
The planning process begins with an analysis of data (scores, structural and causal analysis, and non-cognitive indicators). **(Data-driven)**		
The plan establishes specific student performance goals as the purpose of planning. **(Proactive)**		
Analysis of data trends supports a search for relevant "best practice." **(Research-based)**		
Action plans are developed to establish how and when goals will be reached. Activities relate directly to improvement goals. **(Consistent)**		
A time/task calendar is created to expected completion dates and individual responsibilities. **(Scheduled)**		
All action plans include enabling, implementing, and evaluating plans to encourage successful implementation. **(Implementable)**		

Planning System

Self-Evaluation	Self-Assessment (1–10)	Priority (1–5)
The plan includes regular monitoring, review, and revision. It allows and encourages adjustment as needed. **(Flexible)**		
The plan is published and communicated to all stakeholders. Parents and students are aware of critical plan elements. **(Known)**		
The plan is read by all staff/stakeholders and translated into personal action (tactical) plans. **(Translated)**		
Planning is ongoing. Review and evaluation initiate the next planning cycle. **(Continuous)**		

Curriculum System

Self-Evaluation	Self-Assessment (1–10)	Priority (1–5)
Our school curriculum was designed with "best practice" in mind.		
The school has unpacked state, national, program, and test standards and used these to establish a sequence of grade-level expectations.		
The school has analyzed the expectations and identified the capacities and learnings critical to proficient performance at each grade level.		
All teachers have integrated the exit expectations into the unit and lesson plans. All learnings and competencies are addressed.		
Analysis of the curriculum will show the progression of learnings from initial student status to end-of-year expectations.		
The school's plans and purchases (PD, materials, programs, equipment, and technologies) are driven by student learning and performance needs.		
Staffing decisions reflect identified student learning needs. Issues of style, access, preparation, and experience are addressed.		
All teachers have been trained to develop standards-based units and lessons and to address effective student work patterns in those plans.		
End of year and unit tests are developed before teaching to establish the performance expectations that will drive units and lessons.		

Curriculum System

Self-Evaluation	Self-Assessment (1–10)	Priority (1–5)
The school has profiled all students to address learning needs better and to provide equity in access, experience, and opportunity.		
The unit and lesson plan models are designed to focus on and support active engagement and effective work from all students.		
Lesson plans emphasize the end of unit expectations and prepare students to perform proficiently on the unit test.		
The school's data management system enables teachers to assess the progress of each student and relate student work to student product.		
All student work is analyzed for structural and causal patterns used that were to drive the next planning set.		
The school provides adequate time for teachers to develop, monitor, and refine the curriculum.		
The school publishes and shares curricula among teachers, levels, grades, and departments.		
Review and revise the curriculum.		

04

THE OPENING OF SCHOOL PERIOD

Description: The Opening of School Period (or, more simply, the Opening Period) focuses on getting the students ready for success in school. It emphasizes the need for student work experiences that prepare the student for the learning and performing work that will enable their growth as learner and performer.

Timeframe: The Opening Period begins two weeks before the opening day and lasts through the third week of school. If necessary, it can be extended to make sure the classrooms open successfully.

Goals: The goals for a successful Opening Period focus on establishing expectations, orienting and enculturating students, and building a core of academic and management rituals and routines that will enable all students to be successful.

Priorities for Academic Leaders:

- Make sure that all systems are working as designed.
- Develop observation tools.

- Visibly support teachers and students from arrival to exit and monitor any individual teachers or students that are struggling or obviously not in-tune with the vision.

- Visit all classrooms during instruction time, looking for management and academic rituals and routines, teacher/student rapport, student engagement, etc.

- If problems are identified, meet daily with the leadership team to form contingency plans (plans B and C and so on).

Priorities for Teachers:

- Establish a growth-oriented, student-friendly culture and climate for the classroom — establish rapport with students.

- Introduce and practice daily all schoolwide and classroom academic and management rituals and routines.

- Collect initial data points on students as learners and performers.

- Identify all students who have "at-risk" characteristics and begin addressing the support needs of those students.

- Practice the learning work that will be a foundation for working in the Formative Period and critical to the beginning of the "deep" learning process.

- Introduce the first content for the year and monitor student attention, acquisition, and level of engagement.

Priorities for Students:

- Attend school daily.

- Practice and master all rituals and routines.

- Identify school programs that match interests and talents.

- Participate in curricular and extracurricular activities that are available at the beginning of school.

The summer ends, and students return to school, but they aren't the same students who left at the end of the last school year. They are older, and they have had new experiences — both positive and negative. Some have started to change physically. All the issues, strengths and weaknesses, and performance gaps between and among groups that existed at the end of school will come back to school with them — along with a whole new set.

Unless we have an intentional program for students to carry them through the summer, most will have lost performance and forgotten much of what they knew at the end of the last school year. The important point for the Opening Period is that we have a three- to five-week window of opportunity. During this time, we must create a learning environment that enables all students to overcome the personal and institutional barriers they face and to prepare them with the skills and routines that will support proficient learning.

Opening Period Readiness Self-Assessment

Best Practice Indicators	Yes/No	Priority
The building, grounds, facilities, and classrooms have been checked and are safe and in good working order.		
The staff has agreed to promote a school-wide climate and culture that is safe and welcoming for all students.		
All classrooms have been equipped with the texts, visuals, materials, and technologies needed for the teachers to engage all learners.		
All students have been placed with teachers who are able and prepared to develop them as learners and performers.		
Teachers have received professional development and facilitated planning assistance that prepares them to address learner needs in each period of the Learner Year.		
Initial data profiles of students have been distributed to teachers, and diagnostic tools and formative activities have been planned to enhance the learner profile.		
Students who have exhibited at-risk characteristics have already been identified, and support systems are in place.		
Parent information nights and practical parenting classes have been presented or are planned for the first weeks of school.		
Academic leaders have created observation checklists to be used in monitoring the implementation and impact of the opening of school tactical plans.		

For teachers, several priority issues need to be accomplished before the students arrive. Housekeeping is an important issue. Classrooms need to be ready, all technology needs to work, and all instructional materials need to be available and in good order. Teachers need to complete their class rosters and gather what data they can to identify "at-risk" factors, strengths and weaknesses of each student as a learner, and the strengths and weaknesses of each student as a performer. These datasets should enable them to have an idea of the priority needs of students and the opportunity to plan to meet those needs on day one.

It's also critical that teachers plan the opening units of the year to address more than just content. The opening unit or units should have a formative element that enables teachers to generate baseline data on student performance with learning and performing skills and add that data to the student profile. The units should have ritual and routine elements built in to establish the behavior management rituals and routines that enable best practice behavior, as well as the academic rituals and routines that will allow student success. Teachers then need to plan teacher work, student work, monitoring and collection of student data, and initial planning for student support. Teacher work in the opening of school is critical but not, in itself, enough.

Identifying the types of work that are needed to get students to a point where they can be proficient learners is an essential piece of the planning work required of teachers before school starts. Determining student readiness for the start of school is a significant part of this planning.

We know that successful students exhibit specific characteristics:

- They attend school regularly (five days or less absent without serious cause).

- They behave in ways appropriate to their grade level and follow established rituals and routines (fewer than two referrals in a year).

- They can control attention and stay engaged in learning work for a grade-appropriate period of time.

- They are active listeners and critical readers (they can do acquiring work from oral and written presentations).

- Their reading competencies are appropriate for the grade level (reading rate, oral fluency, and comprehension).

- They are independent thinkers and problem solvers (can initiate thinking and problem solving without direct teacher instruction).

- They can communicate thinking and conclusions orally and in writing at grade-appropriate levels.

- Their content knowledge base is sufficient to support an immediate introduction to this year's content.

Ed Directions' coaches use several tools to compare student profiles to the characteristics of proficient students. The initial profiles that were included in the previous chapter can be updated and identified support needs can be targeted more precisely. Ed Directions' coaches use them in mini PD sessions to get teachers talking about what their goals for the Formative Period need to be. The coaches encourage teachers to use them in designing student work in each unit that will build proficient characteristics in all students in their class or classes. These tools are flexible and are used by the Ed Directions coaches through the Calibrating Period.

Our coaches like to say that we have to *open* school when the students show up, but we have the option to *begin* school earlier than that. Our development of the "rhythm" of the Learner Year indicates that there are optimal times, acceptable times, and inappropriate times for activities. Outreach programs to students and parents, effective parenting programs, and orienting programs for students and teachers — especially new students and teachers — are optimal activities in the two to three weeks before school starts. In the first week of school, these activities can still be effective, but after the third or fourth week of school, their impact on shaping perceptions, attitudes, and culture is negligible. Identifying practices and activities that encourage and enable student success and then implementing in an optimal period maximizes their impact and builds a foundation for the next phase of the Learner Year.

Student work in the weeks before the official opening of school isn't critical, but it can be very beneficial. Effective student work can involve "enculturation" or learning the school culture and climate in a controlled setting and bonding with teachers and administrators through activities that produce teacher/learner teams. It can also involve orienting work that introduces students to the building, their location in the building, and available facilities. Orienting can also include introductions to types of work, elements of the curriculum, and expectations for student growth over the year.

TEACHER/LEARNER PRIORITIES FOR THE TWO WEEKS BEFORE SCHOOL STARTS

These priorities include:

- Introductory and orienting activities.
- Marketing effective activities for role groups — administrators, teachers, students, and parents.

- Building access to students and establish an effective teacher/learner rapport.

- Collecting initial data on students who "at-risk."

- Initiating learner experiences that support learner work once the class starts (e.g., attending rituals).

- Identifying students who lack access, are alienated, or have an adversarial relationship to authority.

- Establishing work and performance expectations.

- Jumpstarting critical reading, thinking, and writing.

The Pre-Opening Period provides teachers with an opportunity to collect data on their students and then connect that data to real live people. Districts and schools collect many of the data points that indicate which students will be successful and which will struggle.

One data stream that is particularly valuable during this period is data that relates to "at-risk characteristics." What "at-risk" means differs from state to state and sometimes from district to district. There are, however, some characteristics that are common to all school settings. The Ed Directions coaches use the tool below to collect data points that have both schoolwide and classroom implications to help establish the magnitude of these issues schoolwide and in individual classroom situations.

SCHOOL DASHBOARD FOR "AT-RISK" INDICATORS

Lack of Academic Success

Critical Group	Number	School Plan This Year
One year behind core group		
Two or more years behind core group		

Discipline

Critical Group	Number	School Plan This Year
Multiple serious offenses		
Multiple class-room disruptions		
Multiple tardiness		

Attendance

Critical Group	Grade	Grade	Grade	School Plan This Year
1 to 5 days				
6 to 10 days				
11 to 20 days				

Performance

Critical Group	Grade	Grade	Grade	School Plan This Year
Scored a "1" in one content area				
Scored a "1" in more than one content area				
Has never scored above a "1"				
21 days or more				

Note: a "1" would be the equivalent of the lowest score a student can make on a state test.

With this data in hand, school administrators and teachers can begin filling out the initial profile on each student and plan support systems that meet the identified needs of students. This initial profile, which was mentioned in the previous chapter, can help teachers decide where to start as they begin the process of building proficient learners and proficient performers and covering the required standard expectations.

"Success Indicators" – Initial Student Profile

Positives

Characteristic	Yes
Independent	
Attentive	
Long-term memory	
Critical vocabulary	
Format master	

Concerns

Characteristic	Yes
Attitude problem	
Attention problem	
Work-ethic problem	
Informal language	
Endurance problems	

Positives			**Concerns**	
Characteristic	**Yes**		**Characteristic**	**Yes**
Critical reading			Negative peer group	
Critical thinking			Little home support	
Critical writing			Impulsive	
Operational vocabulary			Behavior problem	
Successful experience			Low expectations	
Good attitude			Little language experience	
Good work ethic			Low self-esteem	
Positive self-perception			Negative peer group	
Revises work			Attendance problem	
Supportive home			Easily led astray	
High expectations			Demands attention	
Positive peer group			Physical/Mental issues	

Additional metadata on this student:

_____

_____

_____

Effective activities for the Opening Period usually involve stake-holders interacting with each other in ways that establish positive working relationships between and among groups. By interacting with students and introducing them to the administrators, the building, and each other, teachers can prevent added stress and inefficiencies once the doors open. Meeting parents in "neutral" activities provide an opportunity to build a relationship before an incident creates an adversarial situation. It also allows school staff to provide "effective parenting for learning" strategies to parents who may or may not have been successful in school themselves. Shared learning or challenge experiences involving teacher and student teams can help build rapport and access before the students enter the building and experience the classroom culture. Teachers can use the Opening Period to begin an introduction to academic and behavioral rituals and routines in an environment that is not formal or threatening.

One imaginative principal provided a field day for teachers and their classes that included not only breakfast and lunch but also challenges and competitive activities. One of the challenges involved the students preparing their teacher to compete against other teachers in playing a videogame. The principal used the students' frustration over their inability to get teachers to a "proficient" level. (The winning teacher scored only 1,000 points when even inept students scored 500,000.) They ended the day with a discussion by teacher/student teams about how the teacher could have been a better learner. Each team developed a list of "better learner" behaviors that they shared with the rest of the school.

Building stakeholder vision about effective relationships and expected outcomes for the year — success for all students — can create a perception amongst all stakeholders that the school is a safe, welcoming, and student-oriented institution.

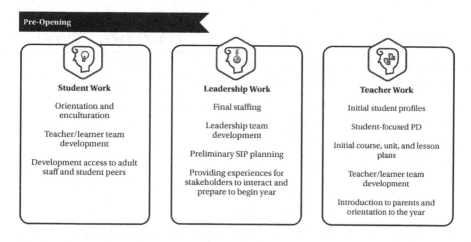

Pre-Opening

Student Work

Orientation and enculturation

Teacher/learner team development

Development access to adult staff and student peers

Leadership Work

Final staffing

Leadership team development

Preliminary SIP planning

Providing experiences for stakeholders to interact and prepare to begin year

Teacher Work

Initial student profiles

Student-focused PD

Initial course, unit, and lesson plans

Teacher/learner team development

Introduction to parents and orientation to the year

Once school officially starts, the Opening Period clock begins to tick. Administrators and teachers will have three weeks (maybe up to five) to get the students ready to be successful. Getting this done requires prior planning and practice by the adults. Much of the success or failure after the first three weeks of school will be determined by the students' perceptions of the school as safe and welcoming, of self as successful learner and performer, their relationship with their teacher(s), and of their learner work.

Leadership Readiness – Are We Ready for Them?

Readiness Checklist	Completed and Ready	Priority
School facilities have been checked and are functioning. All safety issues have been resolved.		
Support systems — e.g., bus patterns — have been audited and are working effectively.		
Staffing has been completed. All instructional and support staff have been hired and have been prepared for the opening of school.		

Readiness Checklist	Completed and Ready	Priority
The school plan for the Opening Period has been marketed and turned into tactical plans by all staff.		
Teachers have plans for developing "best practice" climate and culture for their classrooms.		
Teachers and staff have practiced and standardized behavior management rituals and routines to ensure fair and consistent management of behavior.		
Teachers have developed a plan for academic and management rituals and routines such as including a schedule for practice mastery.		
Teachers have identified institutional and personal "at-risk" indicators that may be barriers to student success.		
Teachers have developed initial profiles for each student.		
All teachers have the opportunity to participate in activities designed to build rapport and create teacher/learner teams.		
Teachers have shared goals and expectations with parents and students.		
Teachers have all the materials and technologies in place.		
Teachers have plans for the development of effective learner work competencies.		
Parents have been introduced to effective parenting and are committed to supporting regular attendance and home-based learning experiences.		
Parents have developed a plan for supporting welcoming activities and congratulatory activities for students and staff.		

Readiness Checklist	Completed and Ready	Priority
Parents have created a "talent bank" that teachers can use to find resources for classroom and extended classroom activities.		
Parents have created a regular meeting schedule focused on the "effective parenting of learners" for each phase of the Learner Year.		
Students have completed the maintenance work provided by the school at the end of the last school year.		
Students have completed the challenge to read a variety of different genres and record their experiences.		
Students have acquired all those things they will need to be present and ready for class every day.		

To open a school that will enable all students to be successful, all stakeholders (administrators, teachers, students, and parents) will have to contribute. Each group has a specific role, and there are optimal behaviors for each of these roles. Leadership must keep the focus on the priority of all the stakeholder groups — student success.

During the week before school starts, administrators need to meet with the leadership team, the academic support staff, and teachers to determine whether or not they are ready for the students to come through the door.

Much of the research Ed Directions has studied relative to work in turnaround schools suggests that building an effective teaching/learning/performing community requires commitment from all stakeholders (school leaders, teachers, students, and parents). It is critical that this learning/performing team be grounded in a culture and climate that emphasizes student commitment to high-level engagement in learning and performing work. The burden of hard work can't fall just on the teachers. Students have to be highly engaged in rigorous work for the learning community to reach its goals.

The goal of "orienting" programs is to establish clear goals for all participants and transparent lines of communication among all stakeholders. To do this in an effective and timely fashion, schools need to plan student experiences during the Opening Period, monitor the implementation of the plan, and assess the impact of the plan on the students in the class. If schools wait until the middle of the first semester for these meetings, the culture, climate, and rapport will already be set (unintentionally) by the interactions that took place during the opening of school.

When students arrive at school, they will be spread out along a continuum of performance from far behind to well ahead. Still, the expectation is that we will move all of them to some level of proficiency before the end of the year. Ed Directions begins our work with a school by helping the staff to come to grips with how students learn, why they perform as they do, and how diversity complicates the learning/performing process. Usually, we will begin with a discussion of the student profiles that teachers developed from the student data that was available to them in the summer and at the opening of school. The initial focus of the discussion includes both the assessment of barriers to success and "at-risk" indicators. For each potential barrier or at-risk characteristic, we emphasize that there are a number of different possible causes.

CAUSATION – BARRIERS AND "AT-RISK" ISSUES

The Ed Directions coaches use a "status check" assessment guide to facilitate discussions between and among role groups and a school. This initial check identifies barriers to success and looks at institutional and personal characteristics that may be causes of the barriers.

Issue Area	Institutional Causes	Personal Causes
Low or Irregular Attendance	• Lack of a proactive attendance policy. • Lack of activities that make school attractive to students. • High rate of suspensions and removal from class. • High rates of teacher absence. • Low expectations for student attendance.	• Low expectations of self. • Lack of family support. • Dysfunctional family issues. • Chronic physical or mental issues. • Transportation issues. • Community issues. • Negative interactions with peers. • Negative interactions with adults.

Issue Area	Institutional Causes	Personal Causes
At-Risk or Dangerous Behavior	• Reactive rather than proactive behavior management. • Behavior management that is perceived as inconsistent or unfair. • Lack of clear chain-of-command for behavior management. • Lack of training in defusing confrontations. • Confrontational and rough desist styles of management. • "Get them out of here" attitudes among staff. • Ineffective student mix in classrooms. • Unaddressed bullying by students or staff. • Unaddressed gang or clique activity.	• Low self-esteem. • Low levels of impulse control. • Failure to accept correction. • Lack of social competencies. • Lack of emotional competencies. • Social and emotional immaturity. • Peer group pressures. • Attention deficit issues. • Escalating engagement response to adults. • Gang or clique membership. • Unaddressed learning issues. • Prior failure in school. • Removal from class, in-school suspension, or suspension more than three times in a year.

Issue Area	Institutional Causes	Personal Causes
Lack of Language Experience or Proficiency	• Common use of language inconsistent with standards. • Programs lacking extensive experience with text in oral language. • Programs lacking experience with real-world language.	• Perception of self as reader and writer. • Prior failure in reading or writing. • Limited life experiences. • Limited engagement with text at home and community. • No life experience in communicating in the formal language of the discipline. • Limited family support for language development. • Delayed language development or language immaturity.
Unsuccessful Academic Experience	• Programs that establish winners and losers and allow students to fail. • Accidental and "one-size-fits-all" support for non-traditional and at-risk learners. • Ineffective classroom management, organization, or student mix. • Focus on content coverage or keeping pace with curriculum guide and not on students' learning.	• Low expectations of self. • Acceptance of personal failure. • Inadequate work ethic and work experience. • Prior academic experience that involved off-level material, work, and language use. • Falling one or more years behind an age cohort group. • Missing five or more days of school each year.

This list is abridged, but it emphasizes that there are both personal and institutional causes. It reinforces the idea that students are different and that we must provide intentional and diverse experiences and supports if we want to move all of them toward the same set of expectations. Given the mandate to move all students to "proficiency" and erase performance gaps between and among groups of students, schools cannot afford to miss an opportunity to eliminate barriers standing in the way of student growth. The initial planning for the year involves identifying factors that create performance diversity and addressing those factors in all lesson plans and support plans during the Opening Period. Eliminating the institutional causes related to underperformance can be addressed during the summer as staff builds climate and culture. However, eliminating personal causes may involve interactions with students in class and students and parents in non-threatening discussions.

TEACHER AND LEARNER TEAMS

The same timeframe applies to the development of teacher/learner teams. Developing shared learning or adventure experiences are useful in building rapport and relationships if done before school starts. If teachers and students can work together before school starts — participating in a shared ordeal or learning experience — they can establish a rapport that will enable them to work together as a team in the classroom. It will take effective teacher/learner relationships if teachers are to lead all learners through the rigorous work needed to build proficiency. If they are bonded as a teacher/learner team before school starts, this activity can be seamless.

This experience can be provided after the students arrive at school but is less effective after school starts. It probably can't be done after the third or fourth week of school without an enormous commitment of time and energy. In schools where there has been a negative or confrontational relationship between students and staff, Ed Directions promotes building programs on "neutral" grounds for parents, students, and staff to meet, learn together, and share experiences. Neutral ground eliminates issues, turf, authority, and alienation that can block the development of the rapport needed for an effective classroom.

LITERATE CLASSROOMS – CONTENT AND TECHNOLOGY LITERACY

State standards require very aggressive levels of literacy. Very few relate to recreational reading or initial comprehension. Almost all involve:

- Critical or purposeful reading.
- Reading and analyzing real-world and informational text.
- Reading and relating different genres.
- Using text features and included visuals to unlock the meaning.

- Responding in writing or testing venues to demonstrate thinking about what's been read.

- Building proficiency in reading, writing, thinking, speaking, and listening.

An overlooked element in the discussion of literacy is the fact that all content tests require critical reading and use of content vocabulary.

Establishing a classroom that builds communication competency requires that the classroom offer opportunities to do purposeful reading of both real-world and academic text, reflect on what is being read or heard, and communicate that thinking in writing or a follow-up discussion. Added benefit would be derived from the opportunity to do active listening to real-world and academic speech.

Building this level of communication or content literacy requires pre-planning and foundation building. Students will need a classroom climate that encourages them to take academic risks and accept a learning experience set that enables them to build the organizational scaffolds or mental models that create meaning for the technical language they are learning. This will become critical in the Formative Period but is most effectively introduced in the opening weeks of school.

CLIMATE AND CULTURE

Developing climate and culture can be problematic. If teachers are not intentional about their development, they will get one that is not intentional. Culture (those artifacts, policies, procedures, and systems that define what the school is) and climate (the tone or atmosphere that culture shows to people) need to be introduced and shaped early in the year if they are going to produce the maximum impact. Our leadership coaches emphasize that if schools don't design and build climate and culture intentionally, the students will create one for the school (and the school probably won't be happy with it).

Early development of culture and climate can begin before school starts, but the optimal time is the first three weeks of school. This is critical. Students need to feel safe, welcomed, and valued when they come to school on the first day. From the time they arrive at school, they begin experiencing the climate and culture of the school and classroom and develop their perception of how they fit into the classroom environment. That is why many of the behavior management programs emphasize that during the Opening Period, all adult/student interactions be proactive and not punitive, involve mutual respect and humor if possible, and establish an etiquette for the interaction of role groups. After the fifth week of school, culture and climate will have evolved, and efforts to change the culture and climate will be negligible unless major schedule or student distribution changes are used to "re-open" the class.

RITUALS AND ROUTINES

Building classrooms that support effective learning and performing for all students is another objective of the Opening Period. Like climate and culture, these can be planned during the summer, but the optimal time for development is in the first two weeks of school. During this time, teachers and students need to build a rapport that emphasizes mutual respect and commitment to high-level engagement and effective work. All students must develop a shared collection of core competencies that will enable all students, even those whose profiles indicate barriers to success, to be successful at learning and performing. This requires the introduction and mastery of behavior management and academic rituals and routines.

Management routines can be punitive (focused on reacting to inappropriate behaviors) or optimal (focused on proactive learning behaviors). Shaping behavior in the classroom toward optimal learning and performing behaviors has a far more significant impact on shaping student attitude and perception about school than harsh punishment for inappropriate behaviors. Management rituals and routines are essential. They need to be introduced immediately and practiced so that they are mastered in the first two to three weeks of school. Our leadership coaches like to remind teachers that if they don't have students master their management rituals and routines, they will have students who will misbehave on a regular basis and students who will never reach their potential as learners or performers.

A sampling of behavior management rituals includes:

- Entering school protocol
- Exiting school protocol
- Transition between classes
- Lunchroom rituals – going, eating, and returning
- Responding to directions for transitions
- Entering class
- Bell ringer activities
- High-level engagement
- Following classroom behavior expectations
- Following adult/student interaction etiquette
- Responding to criticism or correction
- Exiting class
- Assemblies/athletics – going, participating, and returning
- Demonstrating optimal learning
- Dealing with serious or threatening situations

Behavioral management rituals are important, but research indicates that they can be positive or negative. Behavioral rituals that emphasize optimal learning behaviors support a positive classroom climate and acquisition and use of academic rituals and routines. Optimal behavioral rituals support interactions between and among groups and help students develop emotional and social competencies that are critical to success in school. Behavioral rituals that are reactionary and punitive create an adverse classroom climate, inhibit the development of a positive teacher/student rapport, and provide an opportunity for the worst elements of emotional and social intelligence to come into play.

Academic rituals and routines are also critical and should be introduced early and practiced until they are mastered. These rituals and routines establish the expectations for the student work ethic, develop an understanding of high-level engagement in learning work, and establish the types and sequence of work that will be expected of learners and performers. In "best practice," there are several types of rituals and routines. Some are school-based and expected of all students in all classes. Others are grade-level expectations and can differ between grade levels and should escalate as students move through the grades. Others are related to specific disciplines of study. Some are classroom-specific and represent rituals and routines that are particular to the teacher or students' needs.

Academic rituals and routines support the development of learning competencies, independent growth, thinking competencies, and the organized acquisition of learning. They are fundamental to building discipline-specific language in all students and helping erase the "success gap" that is a result of unequal life or language experience.

A sampling of academic rituals — those that facilitate the teaching/learning process and those that support effective learning — follows.

Academic Rituals

Rituals That Facilitate Classroom Work

- Entering class
- Turning in homework
- Starting class work
- Work engagement
- Asking questions
- Answering questions
- Changing activities
- Submitting work
- Changing materials
- Listening to a speaker
- Viewing a video
- Sustained silent reading
- Conducting research
- Performing an experiment
- Participating work or learning groups

Rituals That Support Effective Learning

- Active listening
- Note taking
- Translating learning
- Creating meaning
- Reading to learn
- Using discipline language
- Organizing materials
- Writing in response to reading
- Writing in response to thinking
- Revising work to meet a standard
- Writing to learn or to organize learning
- Using a rubric to self-assess
- Revising to proficiency
- Participating in question and answer sessions
- Participating in group discussions

Within the academic rituals and routines, there needs to be a focus on the core competencies of learning and performing. Teacher and student work, content coverage, and formative assessments need to include, focus on, and monitor critical reading, critical thinking, and purposeful writing. In the next period of the Learner Year — the Formative Period — it will be vital for students to take the learning they acquire, organize it, and store it in a way that creates meaning in long-term memory.

Developing intentional unit and lesson plans enables mastery of rituals and routines, effective student work, and building the competencies needed for success. Student engagement, rigorous work, and ongoing monitoring of student growth enables teachers and administrators to provide targeted support and are very effective tools in shaping student attitudes and perceptions. If initiated in the Opening Period, they have the maximum impact that can continue to have a positive effect through the Formative Period. If teachers can build a success-based culture and climate, establish a rapport with their students, move all students toward mastery of critical rituals and routines, and engage the students in effective student work experiences, they will have classrooms that work.

This means that students need to become acquainted with all the different levels of learning that lead to proficiency. In the Opening Period, however, two levels are critical to developing mastery of the other levels in the Formative Period.

First, students need to learn how to *attend*. At a minimum, they need to become active listeners and critical readers. Without attention, there can be no learning. Next, they also need to learn how to *acquire* those things that must be learned. At a minimum, they need to learn how to take notes from teacher delivery, from readings, and from technology resources. Unless the students do some work to acquire learning, long-term memory and use of what is learned will not be possible.

If teachers fail to develop the attending and acquiring competencies required for effective learning, they can do a wonderful job of planning a lesson only to have students fail to learn or learn only those things that fall into their attention zone.

OPENING SCHOOL – EFFECTIVE STUDENT LEARNING WORK

Attending Work:

1. Are there attention problems in my class?

2. Do I need more than one attending strategy?

3. Will multiple opportunities to attend be needed?

4. How will I hold students accountable for attending? What data will I collect?

Acquiring Work:

1. Are there acquiring preference differences?

2. Do I need differentiated or tiered work?

3. Will my class rituals help?

4. Is homework an issue?

5. How will I hold students accountable for acquiring? What data will I collect?

By the end of the Opening Period, all students need to understand that for the school to turn around, student performance needs to turn around. They also need to understand the teacher work is not the critical element in turning around student performance. High-level engagement by students in effective learning work is the most critical element of the Opening and Formative Periods.

UPDATING STUDENT PROFILES

One critical piece of teacher work must be done through the entire Opening Period. Teachers need to collect cognitive and noncognitive data points on student work to inform their decision-making and planning so that all teacher and student work can be intentional and targeted to the specific students in the classroom. The Opening Period student profiles need to be updated weekly as more student datasets become available. PLC discussions need to change to utilize the new data streams in making more informed decisions about lesson planning and providing support and remediation for students.

Teachers need to know which students cannot read to learn or cannot take notes. They need to know which students are learning and which are not. They need to see the level of student thinking and the maturation of student thinking. They need to establish a baseline understanding of student emotional and social competencies and of the student's ability to do critical reading, writing, and thinking. Some of this information can be generated through diagnostic assessments, while other information will have to be collected from anecdotal and observational data. The data must be collected, however, because for a teacher or leadership team to develop an intentional curriculum, they have to know both where they are going and where the students are currently.

Most effective leadership programs emphasize the need for leaders to build and market a collective vision of what their organization is. By the end of the Opening Period, Ed Directions likes to see all stakeholders bought-in on a shared vision of where the school is and where the school is going. That is to say, perspectives on student work, effective cultures and climates in place, academic and behavior management rituals and routines practiced and mastered, optimal learning behaviors set and in place, and the initial learning work routine established.

Teachers share responsibility for building and marketing a shared vision of a successful classroom. In the Opening Period, teachers and their students must share a vision of an effective class.

ACADEMIC LEADERSHIP – MONITORING IMPLEMENTATION

At the end of the third week of school, leaders and teachers will have to judge whether they have opened school effectively. If any of the essential elements are missing, the staff cannot build classrooms that will move all students to proficient learning and performance. If they do not have these elements in place, they have not completed the opening of an effective teaching/learning center and need to extend their opening work until they get these elements in place. At one school, our coaches encountered a staff that was still trying to open the school in December and had missed their opportunity to grow student potential during the whole of the Formative Period of the Learner Year.

For school leaders, the Opening Period provides the first real opportunity for data collection on what works and what doesn't, and who works and who doesn't. If teachers are not doing best-practice opening work, they need to be identified and conferenced/remediated immediately. If they have not completed the opening work of setting climate, culture, rituals, and routines in their classrooms, this puts students at-risk and endangers the school turnaround process.

School leadership also needs to be active in observing student demonstrations of rituals and routines and providing shaping feedback. If students are not complying with rituals and routines, they not only risk their opportunity to be learners, but they can put other students and whole classes at-risk as well. Behavior, engagement, and student response to intervention need to be monitored, and behavior modification assistance must begin as early as possible. Part of this process may require redistributing students who cannot or will not fit into a classroom culture. Class lists are not set in stone. Students can and should be moved when necessary to improve the teaching and learning environment.

We see weeks one and two of the school year as the most important of the whole year. While you cannot make the year successful in weeks one and two, you can ensure that it will be unsuccessful if you do the wrong things during this period.

For administrators, the first week of school can test endurance. Administrators need to monitor all systems to make sure they are working as advertised. Faulty bus routes, staffing issues, or missing or incorrect instructional materials can cause classes to lose beneficial enculturing work in the first week of school. Administrators and school academic leaders also need to be in classrooms daily to make sure that teacher work and student work are valid and consistent with the school plan for the Opening Period. Inappropriate work or ineffective work by either teachers or students must be immediately identified and corrected.

Administrators also need to collect learner and performer data to inform decisions about student placement and support systems for at-risk students. Academic leaders need to be available in PLC discussions to help focus those discussions on student needs and use those discussions to drive informed decision-making and ad hoc planning.

WEEK-BY-WEEK BREAKDOWN OF OPENING OF SCHOOL

Week 1

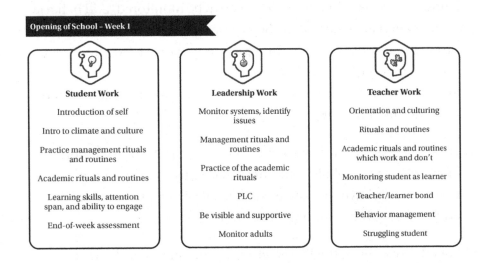

In the first week of school, teachers must establish the climate and culture of their classroom, practice elements of climate and culture, and make sure that everyone understands the expectations, rituals, routines, policies, and practices that will be used in classes.

In addition to building the climate and culture, there are several other teacher priorities:

- Teachers need to introduce the students to the types of teacher work and assessments that will be used to develop them as learners and performers and monitor their growth.

- Teachers need to introduce the content for the year, model performance expectations, and have students practice the types of student work that will be expected as students learn.

- Students must be introduced to and begin mastering and demonstrating mastery of behavior rituals and routines and learner rituals and routines.

- Students must successfully attend and acquire sample learnings. If they cannot attend and acquire independently, they will need to have support in class from either the teacher or from peers to be successful at attending and acquiring. This is fundamental to all of the other learning work that is going to occur during the year.

During the first week, students need to get to school, get to class, and give some effort to the work that is provided for them. They need to give good faith practice to rituals and routines and to the types of learning work that they are going to do. This class culture-building work is the key to the individual student being successful in class and to the teacher's goal of making all students successful and erasing performance gaps. In week one, it is also crucial for students to begin communicating in the language of the discipline. Formal language development is one of the tools that can help bridge performance gaps that have been created by life and language experience.

Week 2

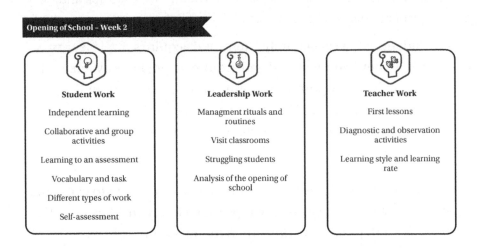

Opening of School – Week 2

Student Work	Leadership Work	Teacher Work
Independent learning	Managment rituals and routines	First lessons
Collaborative and group activities	Visit classrooms	Diagnostic and observation activities
Learning to an assessment	Struggling students	Learning style and learning rate
Vocabulary and task	Analysis of the opening of school	
Different types of work		
Self-assessment		

A successful first week gets teachers and students on track for success. It establishes critical baseline understandings and equips students with behavior and learning strategies and supports for building their potential and demonstrating proficiency.

In the second week of school, the focus shifts from getting school started to mastering the elements introduced in week one. Administrators continue to fine-tune systems and resolve staffing issues but provide more visibility and leadership at the classroom level. It is essential during the second week to ensure teachers are indeed standardizing behavior management and academic rituals and routines and are building a rhythm of teaching and learning that embraces effective student work. Visiting classrooms and acknowledging rituals and routines, shaping those that are not consistent with the SIP vision, and conferencing with teachers who are not building classrooms will enable learning and performing. Validation by leadership is key to successful management cultures.

By the end of week two, administrators should have an idea of what works and doesn't, who's working and who's not. Support for struggling teachers and students should begin by the end of the second week.

In a best-practice situation, all teachers could use the elements introduced in the first week to onboard students to the way rituals and routines fit into building teaching and learning work. Often, the first real unit of study won't begin until the second week, and the student work will be designed to build specific learning skills and apply them to content. In the first unit, teachers need to introduce content and the work students need to perform. This enables the students to acquire those things they have to remember to demonstrate learning.

The goal of the second week of school is to demonstrate to students that the skills they started to learn in week one can indeed make them successful when they must learn and demonstrate learning in the first unit. For this reason, we encourage teachers to use directed learning activities that provide a roadmap that helps the students perform the work proficiently. Here are some examples of students' attending work and acquiring work:

Attending Work – Shapes (Proactive Alert)

1. What did I just say we were going to talk about today?

2. What do you already know about shapes?

3. When I talk about shapes, what are you going to listen for?

4. Okay, we've covered our first shape. In your groups, discuss what you learned. Then, tell me the important things you learned about a square and why you decided it was important.

Acquiring Work – Critical Learnings of a Shape

1. Name:

2. Definition:

3. Drawing:

4. Parts:

5. Formula Set:

6. Examples:

The second week of learning for students involves mastering behavior and academic rituals and routines so that the work that they do can be done in optimal conditions, as well as learning to do effective attending and acquiring work. For students, the goal is to produce a work product that represents their potential as learner and performer and gives teachers a data point in building a profile of each student.

One activity that we use in the second week of school is to begin a unit by giving the students the unit test and then at the end of each student work session, identify the questions on the test that were answered in the student work. This establishes the relationship between the learning work and student accountability for learning. It also begins the introduction of test formats and venues and how they are linked to the types of work that students do in class.

Week 3

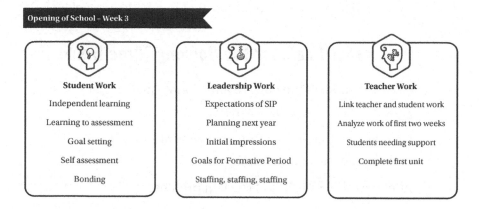

Opening of School - Week 3

Student Work

Independent learning

Learning to assessment

Goal setting

Self assessment

Bonding

Leadership Work

Expectations of SIP

Planning next year

Initial impressions

Goals for Formative Period

Staffing, staffing, staffing

Teacher Work

Link teacher and student work

Analyze work of first two weeks

Students needing support

Complete first unit

By the third week of school, students will have at least a working understanding of all rituals and routines and understand how those rituals and routines relate to their success. They will have had initial experience with directed learning activities and will have an opportunity to demonstrate their learning successfully.

If students have made adequate progress by the third week, teachers can undertake a second unit that allows students to work independently as a learner but also have the product "standardized" by comparing work with a peer group. This approach provides two advantages: The students can work independently, and the teachers can analyze their independence. It also provides support and ensures that every peer understands the learning of the lesson.

Administrators and academic leaders need to use the third week to transition to the Formative Period. This involves discussions with teachers, facilitated planning of the opening units of the Formative Period, and observation plans to ensure regular and timely evaluation of teacher and student work. Administrators need to be visible and active in PLC discussions and facilitate decisions made by PLC groups. The critical pieces of the analysis are the successes and failures of the Opening Period. If the analysis indicates that critical elements for the Formative Period are not in place, the Opening Period may need to be extended for another two or three weeks.

Teacher/Learner Goals for the Opening Three Weeks

- Enculture: Establish the culture and climate needed for students to grow as learners and performers.

- Build a rapport that enables teachers and students to interact in ways that promote competencies.

- Continue work on the initial student profiles.

- Master management and academic rituals and routines.

- Build adult access to students.

- Establish work and performance expectations.

- Build a "literate" classroom and establish a basis for content literacy.

- Jumpstart critical reading, thinking, and writing.

If these elements are not in place or not standard across classes, the potential for student growth in the Formative Period will be diminished. In such cases, the Ed Directions coaches advise extending the Opening Period until the students are ready for formative growth. In one instance, a school was still trying to open a school where all students could be successful in December and never made the transition. The school's scores did not improve.

Weeks 4 and 5

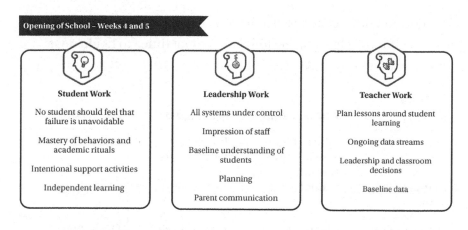

Opening of School – Weeks 4 and 5

Student Work

No student should feel that failure is unavoidable

Mastery of behaviors and academic rituals

Intentional support activities

Independent learning

Leadership Work

All systems under control

Impression of staff

Baseline understanding of students

Planning

Parent communication

Teacher Work

Plan lessons around student learning

Ongoing data streams

Leadership and classroom decisions

Baseline data

If the staff evaluation of the opening of school indicates that the school has not yet achieved the SIP priorities, they can continue opening-style activities into the first two or three weeks of the Formative Period. It is more important that all teachers and classrooms are ready to build successful students, and all students are prepared with core strategies for being successful than it is to cover more content and begin building the formative learning skills. Many times, school leaders will include just a focus on behavior management or academic rituals as a carryover to get that set of competencies in place and then proceed with the Formative Period development.

EFFECTIVE OPENING ACTIVITY – OPTIMAL TIMES

The Ed Directions coaches usually provide schools with a menu of activities for the Opening Period and optimal times to begin developing those activities. An example follows:

Opening Activity	Optimal Time	Acceptable	Importance
Opportunities for parents and students to meet school staff	One to two weeks before the start of school	The week school starts	Desirable
Opportunities for parents and students to see the school building and the classrooms	The week before the start of school	Two or three weeks before the start of school through the first week of school	Desirable
Teacher/ learner bonding experiences	Two and three weeks before the start of school	The first two days of school	Highly desirable
Creating culture and climate	The first five weeks of school	Introduction to some of the program	Critical
Establish management rituals	The first week of school	The second and third weeks of school	Critical
Establish academic rituals	The first week of school	The second and third weeks of school	Critical
Build the core learning competencies required for success	The first five weeks of school	The second five weeks of school	Critical

Opening Activity	Optimal Time	Acceptable	Importance
Convince all students that success is possible	The first five weeks of school	The second five weeks of school	Critical
Elimination of ineffective or disruptive behaviors	The first three weeks of school	The fourth and fifth weeks of school	Critical
Intentional support for students exhibiting "at-risk" behaviors	Two weeks before school starts through first two weeks of school	The third, fourth, and fifth weeks of school	Highly desirable
Collection and analysis of student performance work	First three weeks of school	The Formative Period	Critical
Formative assessments to use the elements of the assessment process	First two weeks of school	Third, fourth, and fifth weeks of school	Critical
Identification of at-risk teachers and students in the development of support systems	The first three weeks of school	Ongoing	Critical
Evaluate the opening of school, extend if needed, and plan for next year	The third and fourth weeks of school	Early-Formative Period	Critical

When leaders plan an effective opening of school, they develop a sequence of activities for parents, teachers, and students that introduce the goals of the year, the expectations of students, and provide an opportunity for parents and students to experience the culture and climate the school intends to promote in the classrooms. They also build staff confidence and competence in building student-focused lessons. The process of planning an opening for student success changes the way teachers look at lesson planning, progress monitoring, and grading.

When leaders were able to get teachers to implement effective opening strategies, build effective rituals and routines that were followed by all teachers and students, and build the fundamental competencies, students became successful, and the management of school became significantly easier. School leadership and instructional staff note that planning the opening changed the atmosphere of the school as well the students' perceptions of both the school itself and their relationship to the school. We emphasize that if any students decide by the third week of school that they will fail, then they will probably fail. If teachers decide that some students will fail, those students will likely fail. If teachers and students believe that all can be successful, then very possibly, they have the best chance to be.

Evaluating the Opening Period

Best-Practice Indicators	Yes/No	Priority
Teachers developed and implemented tactical plans for building the foundational competencies needed for all students to be successful.		
Administrators and academic leaders were visible in classrooms and hallways daily and monitored the implementation of tactical plans.		

Best-Practice Indicators	Yes/No	Priority
Teachers and students who were struggling during the opening were identified and provided with conferencing and support.		
Teachers provided diagnostic activities and use those diagnostic activities to complete student profiles.		
All teachers introduced the learner work expected of students and provided formative or directed practice.		
All students had an opportunity to engage in the levels of work required for long-term memory and mastered attending and acquiring work.		
All teachers used learnings from unpacked standards to create expectations for units and designed lessons around the student work needed for all students to meet expectations.		
Students who are struggling with academic or behavior rituals and routines were identified and provided with immediate assistance and adult support.		
Academic leaders provided weekly feedback to all teachers on observed implementation and impact of tactical plans.		
In the third week of school, academic leaders met with all staff to assess the strengths and weaknesses of the opening of school and developed ad hoc plans to address critical concerns.		
After the first three weeks, no student felt he or she was bound for failure. All saw an opportunity for success and understood what was required.		
The assessment of the opening led to initial conversations about what next year's SIP needs to include to ensure next year's opening is more successful than this year's.		

Opening Period – Planning for Next Year

Timeframe	Concerned/ Action Plan	Leader	Completion Date	Expected Outcome
By End of September				

05

THE FORMATIVE PERIOD

Description: The Formative Period is a time when the focus is on building proficient learners. Content is covered, and students begin learning to use what they learn, but there is a robust "building an efficient learner" strand in the curriculum. With a strong Formative Period, it is possible to improve a student's potential as learner and performer up to a full year.

Timeframe: The Formative Period usually begins after the third week of school, but that can be delayed if opening activities have not been successful. Maximizing growth and potential requires the development of an effective core set of competencies in all students, so it may be necessary to delay the beginning of the formative work. The Formative Period lasts until winter break.

Goals: The goals for the Formative Period focus on making all students effective learners. Emphasis is on the development of formative work habits, high levels of engagement, formative assessments, and independent use of learning. In an effective Formative Period, students become independent learners and independent performers.

Priorities for Academic Leaders:

- Monitor all systems and revise as needed.

- Develop or adapt observation tools for the Formative Period.

- Visibly support teachers and students in classrooms and extra-curricular activities.

- Visit all classes during instruction time, looking for management and academic rituals and routines, evidence of standards focus, teacher planning for learner work, and student engagement.

- If problems are identified, meet daily with leadership team to form plans B and C.

- Participate in PLC discussions and provide leadership in identifying priority needs and building targeted support plans.

- Evaluate teacher/student compatibility and move students if needed to ensure student success.

- Assist teachers in developing Formative Period student profiles by using part-time or retired teachers.

- Collect and analyze data on systems and teacher performance and meet regularly with academic leaders to refine systems and evaluate/support teachers.

- Meet with the leadership team and PLC groups to create a vision of the Calibrating and Testing Periods and begin developing strategies and plans for calibration and assessment.

Priorities for Teachers:

- Fine-tune academic and behavioral rituals and routines.

- Monitor attendance and tardiness and intervene as needed.

- Expand the classroom culture to embrace the use of discipline-specific and formal language in all classroom communications.

- Introduce directed learning and thinking work and build student competency in attending, acquiring, organizing, and creating meaning.

- Embed critical reading, critical thinking, problem-solving, decision-making, and critical writing competencies.

- Provide teacher and peer support to ensure student success, but gradually build student independence as learner, thinker, and performer.

- Develop strategies for purposeful (e.g., reading to learn), critical, and analytical reading.

- Monitor student learning work and update student profiles.

- Provide targeted support for all students not mastering learning competencies.

Priorities for Students:

- Attend school daily.
- Use all rituals and routines proficiently.
- Actively listen and critically read as required in lessons.
- Highly engage in and complete all learning work.
- Give best effort and complete all assessments.

- Participate in pair, group, and class activities.
- Accept suggestions for work improvement and revise work to proficiency.
- Accept support when provided and actively engage in support activities.

The Formative Period can be a period of rapid growth in student knowledge base and performance potential. Teachers can reduce performance gaps and support non-traditional learners when two things happen: First, teachers must be successful in building a learning environment with behavioral and academic rituals and routines that equip all students for success. Second, students start to master active listening, reading to learn, effective notetaking, and prioritizing learnings. If teachers haven't been successful in developing these foundation pieces, academic leaders need to consider extending their opening activities for one or two more weeks. To get maximum growth in the Formative Period, students need to work in an academic environment that prepares them for success.

When Ed Directions is working in a school, we use the checklist below to facilitate discussions with academic leaders and teachers about the school's readiness to begin the Formative Period. If there are more than three "no" answers, we encourage schools to prioritize and pick the top three in terms of impact on students and develop ad hoc plans for those priorities that will be implemented in a two-week extension of the opening.

Formative Period Readiness Self-Assessment

Best Practice Indicators	Yes/No	Priority
The academic leaders' school evaluation indicates that all classrooms have adequate culture and climate so that all students feel safe and welcomed.		
Teacher attendance is maintaining at more than 95 percent, and the school has developed a substitute plan to ensure students and substitute teachers can maintain learning momentum.		
Schoolwide and individual class academic and behavioral rituals and routines have been introduced, practiced, and mastered by all students.		
All teachers have been implementing the district and/or school discipline policies and are promoting optimal behaviors instead of reactionary punishments.		
Observations of classrooms and conversations with students indicate they feel they can be successful and few, if any, students feel they are doomed to failure.		
All teachers are planning around student work and are differentiating for differences and experience base, learning style, learning rate, etc.		
All students have mastered attending and acquiring work strategies and have been introduced to organizing and meaningful work.		
School counselors and support staff monitored student performance as learner during the opening weeks and suggested changes in student distribution and/or support systems provided.		
The academic leadership team developed observation tools for the Formative Period and scheduled regular monitoring of classroom and non-classroom activity.		

Best Practice Indicators	Yes/No	Priority
All teachers who are struggling have been identified, conferenced, and, if necessary, placed on an improvement plan. Academic leaders have scheduled follow-ups to measure the implementation and impact of the improvement plan.		
Students who have exhibited chronic absenteeism or tardiness have been identified, and their attendance has been monitored. Plans are in place to prevent relapse into ineffective attendance patterns.		
Teachers have been trained on effective PLC strategies. Academic leaders have scheduled weekly PLC sessions to monitor student work and growth as learner.		
School data room contains visual reminders of school, grade level, and content area goals and the school's current status in terms of those goals.		
School data room contains samples of student learning work and student performance on assessments that can drive PLC discussions of student growth and special support needed.		

FORMATIVE PERIOD OVERVIEW

In the Formative Period, students must attend, acquire, organize, and create meaning for what they are learning. This daily activity of building long-term memory is critical for making students confident and competent performers later when they are assessed. If we want to grow student potential, we have to develop their proficiency in doing the different types of learning work. This means that we must attend to three different elements of the formative process:

1. **Competencies:** The students must become proficient in using the different types of attending, acquiring, organizing, and creating meaningful work they're going to be required to use in the classroom. They need to learn, for example, how to be active, engaged listeners, and have strategies for reading to learn. They must know how to take notes from listening or reading and prioritize their learnings. They will be expected to understand and use graphical organizers. Additionally, they will have to have strategies for thinking *about* and thinking *with* content. If we require skills from students without first preparing them to use the skills, we have prepared them for failure.

2. **Thoughtful Learning:** A second element relates to the expectation that students become thoughtful learners and responders as opposed to impulsive learners and responders. The meta processes of critical reading/listening, writing/speaking, and thinking must be developed so the students can have multiple opportunities to think about and with content and present their thinking as a part of meaningful learning development.

3. **5 Legged Model**: The third element relates to the attitude, perception, thinking, and experience pieces of the 5 Legged Model. It's essential to the Formative Period that students have work experiences that build the attitudes, perceptions, and thinking required for them to be confident and competent learners.

In most cases, the development of these elements is left to maturation, random academic experience, and life experience. Until about 11th grade, the maturation level doesn't support the levels of thinking we expect of students on assessments and, because many students lack the life experience that develops these characteristics, teachers must include developmental experiences as a part of the formation of the learner. For teachers, this involves providing work that develops the characteristics we want students to own.

Are Staff and Students Ready for Formative Work?

Student Needs — Formative Period	In Place?	Priority
Safe, welcoming environment — Security, confidence.		
Orientation to the building and staff — Positional confidence.		
Enculturation — Successful introduction to culture and climate of the school and classroom.		
Mastery of optimal behavior rituals and routines.		
Mastery of academic rituals and routines related to success.		
Struggling students need to have an individual action plan for addressing at-risk characteristics.		
Access to text and technology materials that enhance learning.		
Unit and lesson plans that are outcome-focused and differentiated for learning and performance.		
Intentional learning work with immediate feedback.		
Progress monitoring and immediate feedback on the quality of student learning work.		
Shaping work that moves student performance from where it was to proficiency.		
All students have access to an adult advocate.		

Student Needs — Formative Period	In Place?	Priority
Trial run experiences for students to test their readiness and informed decisions about support and lesson planning.		
Immediate support for students who are not ready to be successful.		
Assessment opportunities — Regular self-monitoring of growth and current status.		
Teacher/student experiences to build collaborative teaching/learning teams.		

We divide the Formative Period into two subperiods. The first four to six weeks of the Formative Period focus on making all students proficient learners. There are a number of strategies that can come into play in this process. We recommend directed activities to build content knowledge while the students learn to attend or acquire or create meaning for learnings.

FORMATIVE PERIOD: FIRST HALF

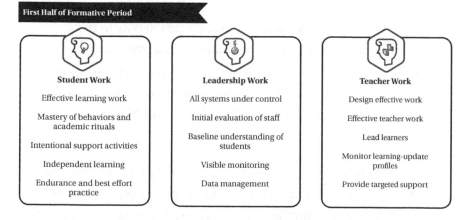

First Half of Formative Period

Student Work	**Leadership Work**	**Teacher Work**
Effective learning work	All systems under control	Design effective work
Mastery of behaviors and academic rituals	Initial evaluation of staff	Effective teacher work
Intentional support activities	Baseline understanding of students	Lead learners
Independent learning	Visible monitoring	Monitor learning-update profiles
Endurance and best effort practice	Data management	Provide targeted support

If students are not ready for the Formative Period, there will not be a Formative Period. The Formative Period is about building each student's potential as a learner. This means the teacher needs to:

- Identify the rituals and routines that all students need to be successful learners.

- Identify those factors that might prevent students from becoming more proficient learners and build an experience set that addresses those priority needs.

If teachers cannot do either the identification or experience building, leadership needs to provide immediate ad hoc professional development and ongoing support for the teachers, for the students, and those teachers' classrooms.

The key to a successful formative experience for all students is the development of a rhythm of student work that enables all students to attend, acquire, organize, and create meaning for all critical learnings and tasks. The work in the Opening Period to prepare all students to attend and acquire effectively makes it possible to begin the development of the effective student work set at the start of the Formative Period — organizing, creating meaning, and assessment experience.

Academic leaders have several important roles to play in the Formative Period. They have to maintain all systems, provide visible support for teachers and learners in classrooms, evaluate teachers — design of teacher work and design of student work — and monitor student growth, update profiles, and redesign student support systems.

Teachers also have to play a variety of roles. They have to continue their role as data manager, PLC participant, progress monitor, and leader of learners. Researchers have indicated specific teacher work strategies are very effective in the early part of the Formative Period.

Ed Directions' coaches use the information sheet included below when working with teachers to plan their work in units and lessons and develop strategies that support student learning and performing.

Formative Period: Effective Strategies for Teacher Work

Work Pattern	Definition	Samples
Maintaining a positive, learner-focused classroom.	Building an effective culture and climate are critical to engaging all students as learners.	Optimal behavior rituals. Individual and class recognition. Daily refining behavior. Learning rituals to proficiency.
Developing lesson plans that identify essential learnings and their link to performance and assessment.	Course, unit, and lesson plans need to reflect the expectations of the standard, the current status of the student, and the learning goals that will move the student to the exit expectations.	Focusing visuals. Proactive tests use. Linking student work to test items. Establishing preparation for different levels of assessment.
Developmental practice with feedback of all rituals, patterns, and strategies with revision to proficiency.	Regularly reviewing the academic and management rituals and routines and the class strategies for complex activities until all students are proficient.	"Timeout. Let's do it again." "What went wrong, and how can we do it better?" "How are we going to do this?"

Work Pattern	Definition	Samples
Preparing quizzes and assessments utilizing the venue, format, and duration expectations of the class and state assessments.	Introducing the various venue, format, and duration expectations so that the student understanding of what's expected is adequate and they can self-assess mastery as they move through the Formative Period.	Introduction to the different types of questions. Providing questions in advance and having the students link their learning to the question. Giving a grade for using a testing strategy as well as for an answer.
Providing regular challenge work to encourage students to expand their endurance, engagement, or best effort.	Students are going to work in an informal comfort zone. We need to alert them that we are going to ask them to work beyond their comfort zone and increase the quality of their "best effort."	Establish for the students their current status. Establish a goal for the challenging work. Provide feedback and encourage "one more step." Wait time and struggle time.
Requiring discipline-specific language for all classroom communications.	Student comfort zone for communication is probably vernacular language. Communication in class needs to encourage the use of discipline-specific language in formal register. This may require shaping work and frequent reminders in the Formative Period.	"Your word/our learned word" activities. Token economy rewards for effective use. Wait time and struggle time.

Work Pattern	Definition	Samples
Building in equity of experience and opportunity in all formative and cumulative work.	All students should get a chance to answer questions, ask questions, and lead a group discussion. Many times, students who do these things naturally dominate the activity, but it's beneficial for all students.	Q and A rituals that don't honor volunteers. Rotating opportunities. Support systems for students who are not comfortable engaging or leading. Trio collaborative work (usually work with three people) with rotating spokespersons.
Structuring feedback loops for students to reduce dependence on teacher input.	By third grade, many students are teacher-dependent responders and teacher-dependent workers. Many need to be weaned from teacher dependence so they can become independent.	Wait time and struggle time. "Ask a student first" transitions. "Trio sharing first" transitions. Independent work with feedback.
Embedding critical reading, critical writing, critical thinking, problem-solving, and decision-making work into lessons and units.	Until tenth grade, most students are impulsive thinkers and responders. Giving them work that requires deep thinking and complex processing builds brain structures that support thoughtful work and thoughtful response.	"Challenge" activities that are more complex than normal classroom work. Problem-of-the-day work. Unit decision-making by individuals.

Work Pattern	Definition	Samples
Building lesson delivery around appropriate "chunks" of learning.	From grades three through seven, students can probably process three to five new learnings at a time. This does not allow enough learning cycles to cover what must be covered. Work designed to build learning chunks expands student potential.	Post activity alerts to define for the student what they learned.

These teaching strategies ensure that all students have equal access to effective formative experiences and have equal opportunities to grow. There is a temptation to teach to the teachable, but in the early part of the Formative Period, teachers must enable all the students in their charge to become effective learners. This means that they have to do more than just plan lessons and cover content. They must build critical learner competencies, build learner confidence, and build a learner experience base that will support proficient performance in the Calibrating Period.

During the Opening Period, teachers focused on preparing the students to learn. The emphasis was on building academic rituals and routines that enabled all students to attend to priority learnings and do work that allowed them to acquire those learnings. In the first half of the Formative Period, students need to expand their work experience to embrace all of the other levels of work that take learnings from awareness to meaningful storage in long-term memory.

This means that teachers have to expand student work so that each day, critical learnings are attended, acquired, organized, and made meaningful. These work experiences are common to all periods of the Learner Year but will differ from period to period in focus and rigor. The Ed Directions coaches use the information chart below to facilitate the development of the four levels of work in the Formative Period.

Formative Period: Types of Student Work

Work Type	Why it is Important	A Problem Causes
Attending Work	Critical listening and reading are fundamental to acquiring the learnings embedded in classroom work. Critical listening is a taught skill essential for students to take notes from the lecture, and critical reading enables them to read to learn or read for assessment. It is crucial for students to use textbooks efficiently and to understand both the question and any data included in the question.	Without effective listening and reading skills, students can fail to identify what has to be learned and prioritize what work must be done. Without these two skills, students can remember what they find interesting but miss what they have to learn. Few lacking the skills will be able to identify the critical vocabulary learning set or a lesson.
Acquiring Work	Acquiring and Practicing work requires a student to take notes, journal, or in some other way to record what has to be learned, why it has to be learned, and what the relevant details are.	Without effective acquiring skills, students can record bits and pieces of learnings or unnecessary elements. They can also fail to prioritize the learnings and prepare those things for "deep" learning.

Work Type	Why it is Important	A Problem Causes
Organizing Work	Students must do something with what they acquire if they want to get it into long-term memory. Organizing learnings, linking learnings to tasks or visuals, or elaborating learnings in their own words transfers the learnings from short-term to long-term memory.	Most students do not own effective translating strategies, so they're forced to work out of short-term memory. Most will be short-term memory dependent by third grade. While they will be able to score on a unit test, they will have trouble recalling the learning on an end-of-year assessment and can miss questions even when they "know" the answer.
Meaningful Work	Once information is in long-term memory, it can be used in a variety of different ways. For assessment purposes, it has to be cued in long-term memory to language. This means the student has to create meaning for the learning, including the language cues that will retrieve the learning and memory. Work creates meaning with language and involves thinking about our thinking with the learning. Work that creates meaning includes thinking, problem-solving, and decision-making activities.	Unless meaning is created, the learning will be stored in long-term memory but may not be retrievable with language. Learning cued to a person, an event, or an experience can be stored but not retrievable.

Work Type	Why it is Important	A Problem Causes
Directed Work (Bonus work type)	Directed work is work that is designed by the teacher to build a specific learning or performing competence in students. In directed work, the teacher does the initial thinking and provides a scaffold or structure to guide students in work that builds patterns of thinking and organizing to support learning and performing.	If students are allowed to do learning or performing work that is incomplete or substandard, it can create a comfort zone around this level of work. If they work at this level over time, it will become their default expectation of self, and it will take a concerted effort to erase the non-proficient work patterns and build proficient patterns.

Teachers must change the way they think about lesson planning. Lesson planning has to become more than just teacher-delivered content followed by student practice. Teachers have to expand on the work done in the Opening Period to build on attending and acquiring strategies by adding organizing and meaningful strategies.

Teachers must change the way they think about lesson planning. Lesson planning has to become more than just teacher-delivered content followed by student practice.

This design model offers several advantages. It leads to lesson plans that are centered around the students' learning work needs. It takes students from attending to creating meaning in the same lesson. It also sets the stage for intentional rather than ritual differentiation. Instead of following one model of differentiation (e.g., learning styles), it encourages teachers to look at the students that they have in class and design work experiences that will enable all students to acquire and create meaning for what they are learning.

This differentiation approach is a significant step toward closing performance gaps.

We have worked with teachers to develop activities that are designed to provide specific types of developmental experiences for students. These are called *Directed Activities*. Directed Activities not only shape the way the students learn, but they also help students begin the process of developing mental models or constructs that will later support independent use and application of what is being learned.

Providing Directed Activities ensures that students know how they are supposed to learn and are successful in their first opportunities to learn. In the Formative Period, we begin by providing students with specific instructions on how to learn and perform, and we make sure that they are successful in their first efforts.

This has numerous benefits:

- It builds the base for independent learning.
- It builds perception of proficient learning work and proficient performance.
- It impacts attitude about work in school.
- It builds a foundation for critical reading, critical writing, and critical thinking.

In the Formative Period, it's important to remember that the process is designed to move students from where they are to where they need to be and to raise their potential as learners and performers. We start with baby steps supported with teacher instructions and directions and move toward learner independence.

Designing Formative Work: Planning for Learning

Attending Work	Acquiring Work	Organizing Work	Meaningful Work
Is there sufficient prior knowledge to support learning?	Are there differences in acquiring preference?	Do my students have different preferences for organizing data?	Will I have to use different meaningful work strategies to enable all students to create meaning?
Are there attention problems in my class?	Do I need to provide differentiated or tiered work?	Will I need multiple opportunities, branching work, or differentiated strategies to ensure that all students organize learning?	Are there extremes in comprehension levels in my class?
Do I need more than one strategy to get everyone's attention?	Are my class academic rituals sufficient to engage all students in acquiring?		Will I need multiple opportunities, branching work, or differentiated strategies to engage all students?
Will I have to provide multiple opportunities to attend?	How will I monitor and shape the acquiring work?	Are my class rituals adequate for supporting all students' high-level engagement in organizing work?	Are my class rituals adequate for supporting all students and engaging them?
How will I monitor their attention to make sure it's adequate?	How will I hold them accountable for the acquiring work?	How will I hold them accountable?	What follow-up strategies will I have to use if students have failed to create meaning for what they have learned?
How will I hold them accountable for attending?	What data will I collect?	What data will I collect?	How will I still hold my students accountable?
What data do I need to collect?	What follow-up will I use for students who have not done adequate acquiring work?	What follow-up will I have to use for students who have not organized their work adequately?	What data will I collect?

> In the Formative Period, it's important to remember that the process is designed to move students from where they are to where they need to be and to raise their potential as learners and performers.

Once students have mastered the initial skills, we can build on this foundation to expand their skill sets, monitor their ability to use them independently in classroom activities, monitor the quality of their work product, and measure the impact their work has on performance on assessments and student projects.

In the first half of the Formative Period, our focus is on building the learner as well as learning the content. If we want to get maximum growth, we have to begin the Formative Period by preparing the learner with the skills and strategies they need to be effective learners. In most cases, this involves using directed work that shapes all students' perception of what the work is for, how the work is done, and the level of effort engagement required to do it proficiently.

PLC DISCUSSION: STUDENT TEST PERFORMANCE

Teacher: _____   Date of assessment: _____

Most missed question number: _____

Number of students who missed or got less than full credit: _____

The question: _____

Question Design Analysis

Type of Question	Qualitative Analysis	Content	Task
Multiple-choice Fill in the blank Short answer Extended answer Response to text or data Real world application Problem solving/decision making Writing prompt Critical thinking or critical reading prompt	Question instructions were clear and concise Consistent with unit goals Rigor was appropriate Discipline-specific language used High-level engagement required Consistent with language and learning work in lessons	Required content was clearly identified Content cues were clear and unambiguous The only knowledge base required for full credit was knowledge of the content and the task	The rubric for full credit was embedded in the question If the task performance was the objective, then the content cues were clear and known Only the task or tasks embedded in the question were required for proficiency

Preparation of the Students for the Question

Unit Teacher Work	Unit Student Work	Purposes of Work	Qualitative Analysis	Relative to the Test
Lecture	Notes	Attend	Consistent with unit and test goals	Consistent with the rigor and content of the correct answer
Worksheet	Workbook	Acquire		
Directed reading	Text questions	Translate	Rigor and duration were adequate	Adequate for building meaning in long-term memory
Class discussion	Reviews	Create meaning		
	Tests or quizzes	Equivalent work	Included complete formative learning set	
Video or visual presentation	Learning log	Shaping work		Adequate to prepare students for the tasks embedded in the question
Guest speaker	Group project	Directed learning or directed performing work	High-level engagement required	
	Problem solving		All learning samples adequate	
		Calibrating work		
			Included differentiated performance	

Sample Student	Answer or Points Earned	Completed Learning Work?	Learning Work Adequate?

By mid- to late-October, teachers should have an idea of how their work must change to be more effective for the students they have in class and how the student work has to change to better prepare individual students for success.

FORMATIVE PERIOD: SECOND HALF

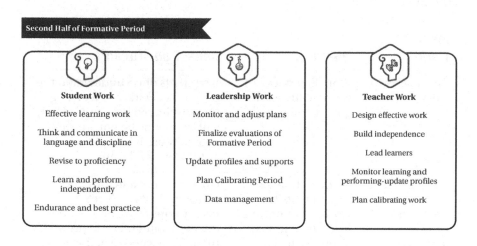

Second Half of Formative Period		
Student Work	**Leadership Work**	**Teacher Work**
Effective learning work	Monitor and adjust plans	Design effective work
Think and communicate in language and discipline	Finalize evaluations of Formative Period	Build independence
Revise to proficiency	Update profiles and supports	Lead learners
Learn and perform independently	Plan Calibrating Period	Monitor learning and performing-update profiles
Endurance and best practice	Data management	Plan calibrating work

In the second half of the Formative Period, it is vital to maintain the rhythm of learning that enables all students to create meaning out of lessons. Effective student and teacher work will still be critical.

Administrators need to be aware of the importance of effective work and begin considering changes in position and/or student distribution if it becomes apparent that a classroom is not developing students as learners and performers.

The teacher's focus on eliminating ineffective practices is as important as providing effective student work and encouraging supportive patterns. We have found that ineffective methods take away time that could be spent on effective student work, establish or reinforce bad habits, and undermine the confidence and competencies of at-risk students. Administrators need to use their monitoring of teacher and student work to identify teachers who engage in ineffective teacher work or who allow students to engage in ineffective practices, determine why they're using the practices, and eliminate the practices if possible.

Formative Period: Ineffective Practices for Student Work

Ineffective Work	What It Is	Impact on Students
Purposeless work.	Work that does not relate to the lesson goals for learning.	If students don't understand the purpose of work, any learning that results can be acquired but will frequently be non-retrievable because it is not perceived as priority or relevant.
Work that is at an inappropriate level or uses an inappropriate format.	Work that causes the students to work below optimal levels or at levels appropriate for lower grades.	Off-level work and formats cause students to develop perceptions, work habits, and comfort zones that will prevent them from working at the levels required by an assessment at the level of expectation.
Work that enables engagement or effort that is below the level required to reach the levels of rigor and endurance of the assessment.	Work that allows students to work below best effort and/or produce substandard products.	Off-level engagement and effort contribute to student underperformance on assessments. For students to become proficient learners, they must be highly engaged in quality work.

Ineffective Work	What It Is	Impact on Students
Work that uses alternative or non-standard vocabulary.	Work that lets students "learn" using language that is not congruent in rigor to the tests.	State and national tests are written in the language of the disciplines. Students are expected to read and reply using the formal language of the discipline. If "dumbed-down" language is a part of their regular classroom routine, they will perform below their potential. Students must communicate in the language of the discipline.
Assessments that include formats and venues that are not a part of the expected standards.	Work that is not formative- does not prepare students with confidence and competence to challenge different types of tests.	It is critical that students master all of the formats, genre, and venues they will face on state and national assessments. Without this practice, they can know the content, but because they are not fluent with answering the different types of questions, they can miss the question.
Submitting imperfect work.	Submitting learning work or performing work that is not proficient (meets expectations) for learning or performing.	When students regularly submit imperfect work, and it is accepted and returned by the teacher, it establishes a comfort zone and a work pattern that the student will take into future work. In the Formative Period, imperfect work should be revised to proficiency to avoid putting students at-risk by accepting substandard work.

The more ineffective student patterns found in the Formative Period, the less formative growth will take place— especially in at-risk students. Late in the Formative Period, administrators and academic leaders need to spend time in classrooms looking for effective and ineffective student work. If ineffective work or work patterns are observed, especially if observed on multiple occasions, teachers need to be contacted and conferenced immediately, and a corrective action plan developed.

The second half of the Formative Period is also essential to eliminate ineffective teacher practices. Ineffective teacher work can undermine the impact of effective student work and exacerbate learning and performance gaps.

Formative Period: Ineffective Practices for Teacher Work

Ineffective Work	What It Is	Impact on Students
Meaningless activity.	The activity for which the students see no purpose. It may involve text questions, worksheets, or practice activities.	Meaningless activities allow students to comply and engage without focus or attention. They do not contribute to the development of habits of mind that lead to independent learning.
Lesson that is beyond student capacity.	Any lesson that involves attention, time, or clusters of learning that are beyond the students' current level of work.	As soon as the students reach their capacity limit, they will start to fall behind and lose the momentum of the lesson. Especially early in the year, this can lead to attitude and perception problems in insecure students.
Practice without shaping feedback.	Students are given practice work that is not monitored by the teacher, and the student determines the level of accuracy and effort that will go into the practice.	Imperfect practice creates imperfect performance. If the students can practice incorrectly five times, that becomes their comfort zone. Only perfect practice creates perfect performance.

Ineffective Work	What It Is	Impact on Students
Activities unrelated to student need.	Activities that are included because they are considered interesting but do not relate to the learning or performing needs of the students.	These activities feed into the student idea that we are doing this to do something. They do little to enhance learning and can cause attitude and perception problems.
Score-driven support.	Support is driven by the student's score and not by the cause of their score.	This can put students into programs that are unrelated to their real needs. Many times, they waste teacher and student time and cause schools to miss the opportunity to improve students.
Unsupervised or unmonitored group work.	Groups are allowed to discuss or engage in learning work without governing rules or supervision.	Frequently wastes class time as students use the time for socialization rather than problem-solving or collaborative learning.

Ineffective teacher work will block student learning gains. It can also take time away from effective students, allow students to establish a comfort zone around the imperfect work, initiate vocabulary that is inappropriate for the level of the assessment, and allow students to develop a comfort zone around less-than-best effort. Some ineffective work patterns cause teachers to build plans and support programs that are unrelated to priority student needs and use up critical time and energy. If academic leaders and teachers want to maximize gains in student potential and make a seamless transition to the Calibrating Period, they have to institutionalize effective student and teacher work and eliminate, to the extent possible, ineffective work.

Ineffective teacher work will block student learning gains.

Ed Directions' coaches use the following observation tool to do quick observations of teacher and student work during the Formative Period.

TEACHER WORK ANALYSIS

Date: _____   Teacher: _____

Period: _____   Observer: _____

Design	Execution	Quality
___ Related to test expectations	___ Lesson plan, critical learnings, and materials ready	___ High quality student and teacher work
___ Focused on student performance expected	___ Lesson goals were posted	___ Mix high quality and adequate teacher and student work
___ Differentiated materials and technologies	___ Teacher started class promptly and made smooth transitions	___ Adequate student and teacher work
___ Differentiated delivery	___ Academic rituals in place and effective	___ Mix adequate teacher work and inadequate student work
___ Differentiated student work	___ Student work was consistent with the lesson goals and involved all four levels of learning work	___ Both inadequate
___ Effective work set included		
___ Monitoring of engagement plan	___ Teacher kept all students highly engaged in work	
___ Checks for learning planned	___ Teacher kept most students highly engaged in work	
	___ Student engagement was monitored, and corrective feedback given	

Notes:

_____

_____

While teachers and students are working to build independent learners, academic leaders need to be visibly supportive of learning in classrooms, monitoring and adjusting formative plans to ensure students' results are those intended, and monitoring to see what works and what doesn't and who works and who doesn't. Programs and strategies that are not working or are having a negative effect need to be selectively revised or abandoned. Teachers who are unable or unwilling to implement the Formative Plan need ad hoc professional development, attitude adjustment, or reassignment.

If our goal is for all students to work in an optimal learning environment and have an opportunity to be successful as learners and performers, then student/teacher combinations that are not working need to be rethought, and students need to be redistributed. After the Formative Period, any ineffective classrooms or attendance or behavior patterns that are not addressed become the academic leader's responsibility.

At the end of a successful Formative Period, all students should be effective, independent learners. In the first half of the Formative Period, the focus is on supporting students. Lesson plans reflect attending work, acquiring work, and organizing work: work types that create meaning as related learning to the assessment.

In the second half of the Formative Period, the focus is on nurturing independence in all students. Long-term use of directed work can build teacher dependence, especially in insecure students. It can create a perception that the teacher can be coaxed into doing the hard work, especially the thinking work required to begin an assignment.

Also in the second half of the Formative Period, we gradually release the responsibility of learning to the individual student to begin breaking the teacher's dependence on initiating student work. The end of the next period will complete this process.

Teachers need to revisit their learner profiles, identify each student who will be at-risk in the Calibrating Period (the next part of the school year), and begin grouping students for targeted support at the beginning of the Calibrating Period.

"Success Indicators" – Student Profile

Positives			Concerns		
Characteristic	**Yes**		**Characteristic**	**Yes**	
Independent			Attitude problem		
Attentive			Attention problem		
Long-term memory			Work-ethic problem		
Critical vocabulary			Informal language		
Format master			Endurance problems		
Critical reading			Negative peer group		
Critical thinking			Little home support		
Critical writing			Impulsive		
Operational vocabulary			Behavior problem		
Successful experience			Low expectations		
Good attitude			Little language experience		
Good work ethic			Low self-esteem		
Positive self-perception			Negative peer group		
Revises work			Attendance problem		
Supportive home			Easily led astray		

Positives			*Concerns*		
Characteristic	*Yes*		*Characteristic*	*Yes*	
High expectations			Demands attention		
Positive peer group			Physical/Mental issues		

Students with more than one "concern" characteristic need to have concerns prioritized and receive support in the concern area from the beginning of the Calibrating Period until the concern has been erased or a successful compensating strategy has been put in place.

Evaluating the Formative Period

Best Practice Indicators	Yes/No	Priority
Culture and climate were effective, and all teachers developed a rapport with students that enabled them to keep students highly engaged in quality work.		
Teachers maintained a focus on developing units and lessons around student work and eliminated ineffective teacher and student strategies.		
All students mastered the work pattern of attend, acquire, organize, and create meaning.		
All students mastered working independently out of long-term and short-term memory.		
Teachers built student confidence to the point where students worked independently within their comfort zones.		
School counselors and coaches used classroom observations to identify problematic teacher-to-student matches and recommended redistribution of students as needed.		

Best Practice Indicators	Yes/No	Priority
Academic leaders monitored student mastery of the critical language and tasks of the standards selected for development and the Formative Period.		
Students who continued to struggle with behavioral rituals and routines and were unable to engage in optimal behaviors were provided with more aggressive interventions.		
Academic leaders provided weekly feedback to all teachers on observed implementation and impact of Formative Period tactical plans.		
Academic leaders monitored teacher performance, identified those teachers who continue to struggle with developing culture and climate, engaging students in effective work, or building effective rituals and routines.		
All teachers used evaluations of student work and observations of students working to update and complete end of Formative Period profiles.		

Planning for Next Year's Formative Period

Timeframe	Concern/ Action Plan	Leader	Completion Date	Expected Outcome
By End of December				

06

THE CALIBRATING PERIOD

Description: The Calibrating Period is divided into two sub-periods. The first focuses on supporting student development as a performer — especially as a test taker. The second focuses on building independent performance, endurance, and the format facility needed to build fluency and alleviate test anxiety.

Timeframe: The Calibrating Period begins immediately after winter break and lasts until two or three weeks before the Testing Period begins.

Goals: The goals for the Calibrating Period focus on building the independence, confidence, and competence needed for all students to demonstrate their potential on a rigorous, complex test.

Priorities for Academic Leaders:

- Monitor all systems and continue to revise as needed.
- Develop or adapt observation tools for the Calibrating Period.
- Visibly support teachers and students in learning and assessment activities.
- Visit all classrooms during instruction time, looking for high-level engagement in effective work, ineffective teacher or student work, escalating rigor in learning work, activities that build fluency, and assessment formats and venues.
- If problems are identified, meet daily with the leadership team to form plans B and C.
- Participate in PLC discussions and begin discussions of optimal test environments.
- Meet with student cohorts to start encouraging and motivating the best effort.
- Monitor classrooms and encourage "bell-to-bell" engagement in learning work.

Priorities for Teachers:

- Begin directing performance work.
- Assess student status — 5 Legged Model status — and support students with areas of weakness.

- Link old and new learnings to assessment formats and venues.

- Increase the rigor and complexity of learning work and performing work.

- Link learnings and assessments to real-world examples.

- Embed critical reading, thinking, and writing, along with problem-solving and decision-making competencies.

- Continue building student independence.

- Gradually increase the level of rigor for each student's comfort zone until it reaches the level expected on the state assessment.

- Provide feedback for student work with revision to proficiency.

- Begin preparing students for state assessments — format, venue, and endurance.

- Provide targeted support for all students not mastering performance/assessment competencies.

Priorities for Students:

- Attend school daily.

- Work independently as learner and performer.

- Actively listen and critically read as required in lessons.

- Highly engage in and complete all learning and assessment work.

- Revise all work to proficiency.

- Self-assess test readiness and seek assistance if needed.

- Take advantage of all school test prep and content support programs.

- Accept support when provided and actively engage in support activities.

For the school to have a successful Calibrating Period, academic staff and students need to understand the purpose of the Calibrating

Period and how student work needs to change. This requires that academic leaders prepare staff and develop plans for the Calibrating Period in late November and early December. It will also be crucial for academic leaders and support staff to update observation and PLC discussion tools. To get maximum gains in student performance, it is critical that all stakeholders understand how their roles change in the Calibrating Period.

Calibrating Period Readiness Self-Assessment

Best Practice Indicators	Yes/No	Priority
All teachers reviewed the end of Formative Period profiles and identified priority student needs.		
All students have mastered all of the standard formats of assessment found on the state assessment.		
Students can stay engaged in complex, rigorous activities until finished.		
All teachers have a plan for increasing the rigor of student learning work and student performance.		
Administrators and academic leaders have revised their observation tools for the Calibrating Period in-class and out-of-class observations of students and teachers.		
Teachers plan transitions for students so the students can move smoothly into the Calibrating Period, focusing on building performance as well as learning.		
With the use of attendance and tardiness improvement plans, student attendance has reached the goal of 95 percent.		

Best Practice Indicators	Yes/No	Priority
Teacher attendance has reached the goal of 98 percent, and when a teacher absence is unavoidable, the school has a substitute preparation plan to ensure that learning momentum is not lost.		
Teachers have plans for supporting students who have not yet mastered the learning work required for effective calibrating work.		
Cohorts of students (e.g., behavior issues, volatile reactions, insecure, or teacher dependent, etc.) have been created and linked to an adult who can work with the students and serve as a "lightning rod" for the students in the cohort.		

CALIBRATING PERIOD OVERVIEW

In the Calibrating Period, students must continue developing their mastery of learning work and continue to learn at high levels. In this period, however, we begin to address elements that actualize the potential of performance we have been building in the students all year. To make all students proficient performers, we must ensure all students are engaged in work patterns that support learning and performance. This means elements of rigor, engagement, endurance, and effort must be targeted in student work activities. It also means the school's data management system must generate information based on an analysis of student product identifying the point and cause of the breakdown in all non-proficient work.

Teachers must address the 5 Legged Model, remembering that if the negative attitude is present after second grade, it should be the number one priority followed by perception, knowledge, thinking, and experience.

In the first half of the Calibrating Period, administrators must evaluate the Formative Period to see how ready teachers and students are for calibration. It's crucial to market the vision of a Calibrating Period to all staff and students and for administrators to be visible in the classrooms, supporting student best effort and student performance. Teachers have to engage students in effective calibrating work and push them to give the best effort, endure tasks, and take on challenges. Students have multiple responsibilities during this period. They are expected to give time and energy to work given in class, review and revise their work to try to make it more proficient, and seek assistance in becoming more proficient.

In the Calibrating Period, four areas of development must be nurtured as a part of the student work planning:

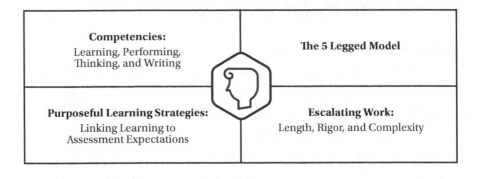

Competencies:
Learning, Performing, Thinking, and Writing

The 5 Legged Model

Purposeful Learning Strategies:
Linking Learning to Assessment Expectations

Escalating Work:
Length, Rigor, and Complexity

STARTING THE CALIBRATING PERIOD

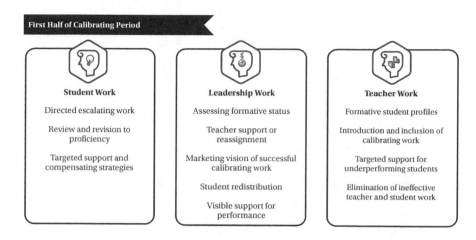

In the Formative Period, we emphasized the need to start students where they are and move them to where they need to be as learners before the winter break. The plan for getting all students to be learners involved student work that enabled them to attend, acquire, organize, and create meaning for things they were learning in class. When a deficit was identified, teachers were encouraged to use directed work — work that not only addressed the content but also built a specific strategy or method for learning the content — and then gradually wean the students away from directed work toward independent work.

Similarly, in the Calibrating Period, it may be necessary to begin with directed activities that increase the level of rigor and duration students have to invest in learning and performing. This escalating or expanding of work builds the experience base students need to be independent performers later in the Calibrating Period.

Calibrating Period: Effective Calibrating Student Work

	Why It is Important	If This is a Problem, It Causes:
Attending Work	The critical listening and reading focus of the Formative Period provides a base for more rigorous and precise attending work in the Calibrating Period. It is crucial students develop not only active reading and listening skills, but also the habits of mind that enable them to read, listen, and learn strategically. Many students listen to prepare their next response, and the communication evolves into parallel monologues. Strategic listening and reading work build the habits of mind that enable dialogue in speaking and writing.	Attention deficits are and will remain an issue in schools. Work that focuses on attending and the habits of mind that support active attention can offset attention deficits. Without effective attending work, learning work does not take place. When students seek clarity and understanding, they start to become literate students defined in state standards.
Acquiring Work	Acquiring and practicing work continues to be necessary, but the level of rigor and endurance must increase if we are going to move all students to proficiency by the time of the test. Additionally, students need to learn to do acquiring work from a variety of different sources and venues. Developing acquiring strategies and expanding the menu of venues from which the students can acquire learning helps build a more independent learner and performer.	Without effective acquiring skills, students record bits and pieces of learnings, irrelevant elements, and miss identifying those things learned. Ineffective acquiring skills can cause a student to develop very slow learning rates and create attitude and perception issues.

	Why It is Important	If This is a Problem, It Causes:
Organizing Work	Organizing work helps get the learning into long-term memory, but it can go into memory in isolation. In the Calibrating Period, organizing work needs to link new learnings to prior learnings. The development of a cumulative perspective for learnings is what separates effective students from those who miss the big picture. State tests will test cumulative learning, procedures, and strategies across disciplines.	In the Formative Period, organizing work was the beginning of the development of a learning pattern typical in effective learners. Unfortunately, that is only part of the picture. Without effective organizing strategies, students tend to learn content as isolated bits of knowledge. Ineffective organizing work can enable learning to get into long-term memory but will not support the linkages needed for the student to see the big picture. Without this big picture perspective, students can learn in class but miss the opportunity to become independent, competent test takers and lifelong learners.
Meaningful Work	Not only does meaningful work enable learning to be retrieved from memory with language cues, it also establishes a framework for retrieval in real-world activities and high-level assessments. Meaningful work then needs to expand in both rigor and focus in the Calibrating Period. The students must do work that not only enables them to find the information but provides a vehicle for them to link information to tasks or situations where the information is required for a solution. Calibrating meaningful work is difficult. Many times, we must prepare and require students to work beyond their maturation level.	Students who fail to create a complete meaningful work set can learn but may still underperform. If the work doesn't create an understanding of the learning and of why the learning is a priority, then students will not have a sufficient learning base to attack challenging questions or real-world scenarios even if they "know" the content.

	Why It is Important	**If This is a Problem, It Causes:**
Calibrating Work	Calibrating work synchronizes a student's understanding of his or her accountability. It establishes the level of rigor, complexity, and duration of tasks students have to engage successfully to be considered proficient. Calibrating work may be learning work, or it may be performing work, but in both cases, it has to be work that expands the student's perspectives and establishes what "best-effort" is expected to produce.	Without effective calibrating, students can learn and can do so effectively but perform well below their potential because of attitude issues, faulty perceptions, inadequate thinking, or inadequate experience working successfully at the level of a task. Without effective calibrating work, it will be very difficult to get students to reach their potential as performers or to accumulate enough points on the state test to be considered proficient.
Directed Work	Directed work is work that is designed by the teacher to build specific learning or performing competencies in students. In directed work, the teacher does initial thinking and provides a scaffold or structure to guide the students in work that builds patterns of thinking and organizing that will support learning and performing. In the Calibrating Period, directed work should include performance work consistent with the format and venue of the state assessment, as well as with the language and level of rigor of the state assessment.	If students are allowed to do learning or performing work that is incomplete or substandard, it can create a comfort zone around this level of work. If they work at this level over time, it will become their default expectation of self, and it will take a concerted effort to erase the non-proficient work patterns and build proficient patterns. Without prior successful experience, students may need directed work to create format fluency, competence, and the attitudes and perceptions needed to endure the task set embedded in the state assessments.

Designing Calibrating Work: Planning for Learning

Attending Work	1. Is there sufficient prior knowledge to support learning?
	2. Are there attention problems in my class?
	3. Do I need more than one strategy to get everyone's attention?
	4. Will I have to provide multiple opportunities to attend?
	5. How will I monitor their attention to make sure it's adequate?
	6. How will I hold them accountable for attending? What data do I need to collect?
	7. How will I escalate their attending work to prepare them for the levels of rigor and endurance required on the state assessment?
Acquiring Work	1. Are there differences in acquiring preference?
	2. Do I need to provide differentiated or tiered work?
	3. Are my class academic rituals sufficient to engage all students in acquiring work?
	4. How will I monitor and shape the acquiring work?
	5. How will I hold them accountable for the acquiring work? What data will I collect?
	6. How will I escalate the rigor and duration of the acquiring work? What data will I collect, and what will I do with it?
	7. What follow-up will I use for students who have not done adequate acquiring work?
	8. What support systems will I need to have in place to make sure that all students acquire the critical learnings?

Organizing Work	1. Do my students have different preferences for organizing data?
	2. Will I need multiple opportunities, branching work, or differentiated strategies to ensure that all students organize learning?
	3. Are my class rituals adequate for supporting all students' high-level engagement in organizing work?
	4. How will I hold them accountable? What data will I collect?
	5. How will I escalate the rigor and duration of the organizing work students do?
	6. What alternative strategies will I have to use to make sure all students have organized their work adequately?
	7. What support systems will I need for students who are struggling with organizing work?
Meaningful Work	1. Will I have to use different meaningful work strategies to enable all students to create meaning?
	2. Are there extremes in comprehension levels in my class?
	3. Will I need multiple opportunities, branching work, or differentiated strategies to engage all students?
	4. Are my class rituals adequate for supporting all students and engaging them?
	5. How will I still hold my students accountable? What data will I collect?
	6. How will I tell if the student work is equivalent and if their performance is adequate?
	7. What follow-up strategies will I have to use if students have failed to create meaning for what they've learned?

Calibrating Work	1. Do I have data on where my students are as learners? Do I know where to start calibrating?
	2. Have I established assessment and EOY expectations to provide a target for the calibrating work?
	3. How will I tell if the students are improving their work as learners or performers?
	4. What data will I collect to inform academic and support decisions?
	5. What alternative strategies for calibration will I use for students who are struggling?

Effective Calibrating Teacher Work

Work Pattern	Definition	Impact on Students
Use of linking and calibrating visuals.	Visuals that support linking learning to prior learnings, assessments, or established rubrics for analyzing work for proficiency.	Visuals serve as a constant reminder of what is important about a particular subject, as well as how we are expected to use what we are learning. Effective visuals in the Calibrating Period help students link learnings, visualize strategies and processes, and develop cumulative understandings of what the year's learnings are about.
Work that links current learnings and prior learnings to different assessment formats and venues.	Work that allows students to link current learnings to prior learnings, assessments, and/or standards. Such work serves as a constant reminder that learning cannot be attained in isolation; it must be seen as a part of a bigger picture.	Linking work enables teachers to revisit prior learnings and take them to new levels or identify the connection between prior and current learning. It can provide the teacher with an opportunity to link what is being learned to unit tests and state assessments.

Work Pattern	Definition	Impact on Students
Student-generated work.	Refers to an activity that takes students out of the learner role and makes them an active participant in the teaching and learning process. It can include designing their organizing tools, writing different types of test questions for what has been learned, etc.	Student-generated work is an effective way to create higher levels of meaning for what is learned. Approaching a set of learnings from the learner perspective builds brain patterns that enable the student to retrieve learnings to a variety of different paths and to independently identify the learning base and tasks they have to perform.
Challenge activities.	Challenge activities raise the bar on student comfort zones. There are a wide variety of challenge activities such as designing rubrics from questions or giving middle school or upper elementary students a high school question to attack. Challenge activities take the student to a new level of learning, thinking, or writing. By the end of the Calibrating Period, we hope that all students can confidently face challenging tasks.	Challenging activities expand student comfort zones. If we challenge learners beyond the level of the assessment, we will have students who have experience working beyond what's expected of them on the state test. Working outside comfort zones not only prepares students for the assessment but sets up transition activities for the End-of-Year Period when we are preparing all students to make a successful transition to the next year. Challenge activities can be used to introduce what next year will be like and can be a part of a cumulative EOY activity.

Work Pattern	Definition	Impact on Students
Self-initiated support activities.	Activities that involve the student in self-assessment, identifying a priority need, and seeking assistance in addressing that need.	Self-assessment and seeking support are important steps in the development of an independent lifelong learner. It is a habit of mind that supports successful transitions and lifelong growth.
Tiered lessons.	Lessons that include simple, expected, and challenging work samples. Tiered lessons can lead to branching strategies, support-based workgroups, and individualized learning analyses.	Tiered lessons ensure all students not only get an opportunity to work successfully with obtained critical learnings, but also develop as deep an understanding of those learnings as their potential allows. This helps the student become a more successful learner and provides the teacher with an ongoing diagnostic of the current status of each student in the learning process.
Rubric-based feedback with revision to proficiency.	The use of an established rubric to analyze student products and provide shaping feedback. The goal is to have the student independently develop rubrics and use them to self-analyze and revise to proficiency.	Rubrics help students understand exactly what is required in an activity or task and gives them a metric to use to evaluate or revise their performance to proficiency. Students who learn to use rubrics answer all the parts of questions, complete tasks, and reshape their perception of learning so that it is adequate for future tasks.

Work Pattern	Definition	Impact on Students
Daily engagement in thinking work, problem-solving, and decision making.	Daily engagement in critical thinking tasks, especially tasks that escalate through the Calibrating Period, prepare students to do independent critical reading, purposeful writing, critical thinking, and problem-solving with confidence and competence.	"Deep thinking" helps build thoughtfulness and establishes multiple access lanes to memory. Thinking tasks escalate, especially if students know how the task is an escalation from what they did before, creating several opportunities for linking learnings, assessments, and standards in the students.
Daily critical reading, writing, and thinking work.	These are tasks that engage students in work that is critical to the development of mature thinking, patterns, and activities. It is important that student reading, writing, and thinking escalate in the Calibrating Period, at least to the level of the assessment. Below-level work will create below-level performance.	Successful students can read, write, and think critically. They have strategies for purposeful and thoughtful development of ideas. Expanding the strategies through different venues and across disciplines can build multiple access channels to learning and enable the students to become more proficient users of memory.

As in the Formative Period, there are ineffective work patterns for students and teachers. These unproductive patterns are more impactful in the Calibrating Period than in the Formative Period and need to be eliminated to the extent possible. They not only waste time, but they can build perceptions and work patterns that undermine learning and performing. For most students, especially "at-risk" students, it is important to have effective, "bell to bell" learning and performing time.

Students – Ineffective Calibrating Work

Ineffective Work	What It Is	Impact on Students
Purposeless work.	Work that is not perceived as relevant to the task required. Students see it as an added but irrelevant requirement.	In the Calibrating Period, purposeless work does not link learning and performance; subsequent use of the learning will not calibrate performance to the levels expected on the state tests.
Off-level work or off-level formats.	Work that includes off-level work and off-level formats, especially if it lacks the rigor and complexity of the tests.	Off-level work and off-level formats cause students to develop perceptions, work habits, and comfort zones that will prevent them from working at the levels required by an assessment at the level of expectation. Calibration to off-level work prepares the students to operate below the level of the test and calibration of performance will be undermined.
Work that enables engagement or effort that is below the level required to reach the levels of rigor and endurance of the assessment.	Work that allows students to work below "best effort." Work that does not develop students to be highly engaged in rigorous work.	Off-level engagement and effort contribute to student underperformance on assessments. If students regularly engage at low levels, don't give their best effort, or don't complete tasks, they will perform well below their potential when the rigor of an assessment requires high-level engagement and effort. In the Calibrating Period, all work should be revised to proficiency.

Ineffective Work	What It Is	Impact on Students
Work that uses alternative or non-standard vocabulary.	Language that is congruent to the language of the state assessment	State tests are written in the language of the disciplines, the state standards, and the test specifications. Students are expected to read and reply using the formal language of these documents. If non-standard language is a part of their regular classroom routine, they will perform below their potential.
Assessments that include formats and venues that are not a part of the expected standards.	Assessment work that is not congruent to the formats and venues of the state assessment.	Students must develop confidence and competence with all the formats, genres, and venues they will face on state assessments. Without this calibration, students can know the content but still miss the question because they aren't fluent in answering the different types of questions.
Submitting imperfect work.	Imperfect work that fails to reach the proficiency levels required for a task.	In the Calibrating Period, students must master task analysis, planning for completion, and revising to proficiency.

During the Calibrating Period, teacher work needs to support high-level student engagement in quality learning and performing work. This means that there are effective "best practices" and ineffective practices for teachers as well as students. For teachers, this includes building an optimal environment for learning and performing, differentiating to maximize the performance of every student, and monitoring student work and student product to provide immediate support for students who struggle.

Calibrating Period: Effective Strategies for Teachers

Work Pattern	Definition	Samples
Use the resources of literate classrooms.	Literate classrooms include supportive visuals, multiple genres related to the content taught, and a variety of equipment and technology related to expanding student understanding.	Cross-discipline, cumulative, capstone, and flow-chart visuals. Computers and other technologies that provide alternative sources of data for students to acquire and interpret. A variety of written or graphic materials that students can use to enhance learning or understanding.
Make the class a learning lab.	Students and teachers should be a teaching and learning team. Design and use lessons and units that enable teachers and students to experiment, take risks, and reverse roles — enhancing both teaching and learning.	Student-developed rubrics. Student as teacher (e.g., videogame with teacher as student). Student-developed test questions and student analysis of test questions and responses.
Provide an optimal learning environment.	In the Calibrating Period, learning work must go from bell to bell. There will not be enough time to do everything that has to be done. If adult or student interruptions break the momentum of the lesson or the rhythm of the learning, we lose our opportunity to escalate student performance.	Effective academic and behavior rituals and routines that are enforced consistently and fairly. Fine-tuning classroom arrangements and student placements in classes. Realigning student/teacher assignments to provide a better match.

Work Pattern	Definition	Samples
Developing lesson plans that gradually increase the level of student learning and performance.	Creating spiraling or expanding strands through lessons and units enables the teacher to gradually increase the rigor of the task and the student's ability to endure the task. The goal should be every student working and giving their best effort by the time they take the test.	Linking work. Vocabulary checks. Tiered and challenge activities. Alternative assessments (e.g., the test is developing a test that covers the priority learnings).
Preparing quizzes and assessments utilizing the venue, format, and duration expectations of the class and state assessments.	Preparing students for different formats, venues, and levels is a vital preparation piece in the Calibrating Period. Identifying how the same content can be tested at third, eighth, and tenth grades can be a very effective way to introduce levels to students. Similarly, selecting different types of multiple-choice, short-answer, or open response questions can prepare students to attack those questions with confidence. By the time students take the test, they should have successfully answered every type of question they will face on the test.	Introduction to the different types of questions. Providing questions in advance and having the students link their learning to the question. Giving a grade for using a testing strategy as well as for an answer. Making a part of the grade the correct identification of the type of question. Having students develop different types of questions as an activity or an assessment of learning. Providing multiple levels of the same question so the students can "challenge up" from where they think they are to the next level of question.

Work Pattern	Definition	Samples
Providing regular challenge work to encourage students to expand their endurance, engagement, or best effort.	Students are going to work in an informal comfort zone. We need to alert them that we are going to ask them to work beyond their comfort zone and increase the quality of their "best effort." In the Calibrating Period, the challenge work can be either in the learning work or in the performing work. This enables the student to be cumulatively successful and then challenged beyond that level. This causes the student to expand the comfort zone and creates an opportunity to reshape attitudes and perceptions, especially perception of self.	Multiple venues or levels of challenge activities for students to select from. Students selected goals on challenge work. Provide feedback and encourage "one more step." Wait time and struggle time. Providing an EOY "ultimate challenge" to provide a focus for students and engage them in a long-term EOY capstone activity.

Work Pattern	Definition	Samples
Provide equity of experience and opportunity in all curricular, co-curricular, and extracurricular activities.	Attitude, perception, thinking, and experience are products of the collective work the student does as learner. If we provide some students with experiences that are beneficial but deny those experiences to other students, we have institutionalized inequity. Every student should have a chance to answer questions, provide leadership, participate in a discussion group, or engage in co-curricular or extracurricular activities that meet their interests and needs.	Q and A rituals that engage all students. Rotating opportunities. Support systems for students who are not comfortable engaging or leading. Trio collaborative work with rotating spokespersons. Variety of co-curricular and extracurricular activities including, but not limited to sports. Leadership training and opportunities for leadership for all students. Student preference profiles that encourage students to identify their interests and talents.
Independent work followed by peer review and independent revision.	By third grade, many students are teacher-dependent responders and teacher-dependent workers. Many need to be weaned from teacher dependence so they can become independent. In the Calibrating Period, independent work may be followed by peer review, but independent work followed by independent revision is critical.	Wait time and struggle time. Trio review with written suggestions followed by independent revision. Independent revision with teacher suggestions if work remains non-proficient.

Work Pattern	Definition	Samples
Linking critical reading, writing, and thinking, problem-solving, and decision-making to assessment expectations—rigor, complexity, and format.	Until tenth grade, most students are impulsive thinkers and responders. Giving them work that requires deep thinking and complex processing builds brain structures that support thoughtful work and thoughtful response. Linking thoughtful response to assessment builds a critical habit of mind and is an essential growth priority for the Calibrating Period.	"Challenge" assessments and assessment-linked activities that are more complex and are revised to proficiency. Assessment task-of-the-day to be task-analyzed and answered proficiently. Self-assessment of critical or purposeful work using a rubric to critique and revise to proficiency.
Building lessons around expanded "chunks" of learning.	Student learning in the Calibrating Period needs to expand in terms of both the rigor and the amount of content processed.	Proactive alert to how many will cluster today. Follow-up work that lets the student complete the creation meaning for the expanded cluster. Clusters need to be linked to assessment expectations — venues and formats.

Ineffective strategies used by teachers in the Calibrating Period can undermine or even reverse student growth even if the student work assigned is potentially effective. Many of these activities are used when teachers are trying to cover content or follow a curriculum pacing guide and lose sight of developing learning and performing.

Ineffective Strategies for Teachers

Ineffective Work	What It Is	Impact on Students
Meaningless activity.	Work that fails to create assessment meaning for students. Work that is not related to assessment format or levels of rigor.	Meaningless activities allow students to comply without relating the learning to performance expectations. This does not contribute to the development of habits of mind that lead to independent performing and can create attitude and perception issues that cause students to perform below their potential.
Lesson that is beyond student capacity or which requires background that the student does not possess.	Any work that exceeds student performance capacity or endurance.	In the Calibrating Period, such work undermines both confidence and competence. It can convince students that they cannot actually succeed on the state assessment.
Work without shaping feedback.	Work that is necessary for formative or calibrating growth must be performed proficiently. Imperfect performance must be revised to proficiency before the students "finish."	Imperfect work creates imperfect performance. If the students are allowed to underperform, underperformance becomes their comfort zone.

Ineffective Work	What It Is	Impact on Students
Activities unrelated to student need.	Work that does not address student priority needs. In the Calibrating Period, all work must be data driven, formative or calibrating, and growth related.	Student need is paramount in the Calibrating Period. Accidental work wastes time and undermines the students' preparation to work to their potential. It breaks learning momentum and limits performance calibration.
Score-driven support.	Support is driven by the students' score and not by the cause of their score.	Relying on scores to plan student support can put students into programs unrelated to their real needs. In the Calibrating Period, student support must be data driven, intentional, and differentiated.
Unsupervised or unmonitored group work.	Groups are allowed to discuss or engage in learning work without governing rules or supervision.	Group work can be an important tool in calibration but if random and unfocused, it can cause confusion about what is being learned and prevent effective performance calibration.

We try to address the issue of ineffective work using the Calibrating Period guide for planning lessons. As in the Formative Period, the guide asks teachers specific questions about their students' readiness for the lesson and adaptations that might be needed to ensure that all students are learners and performers. In schools, the Ed Directions coaches train school academic leaders to use the tool to facilitate teacher lesson planning and to conference with teachers about how they're going to make students better learners in the lesson.

Student work in the Calibrating Period is designed to enable every student to perform to their potential on a cumulative, complex, rigorous assessment. This means that the work has to enable the students to work independently out of long-term memory, give best effort on questions (even if they are both challenging and outside the students' comfort zone), endure the assessment, and complete all tasks and self-assess to see if they can improve the level of work or the precision of the answer.

"Um, is it supposed to work like this?"

CALIBRATING PERIOD: PART 2

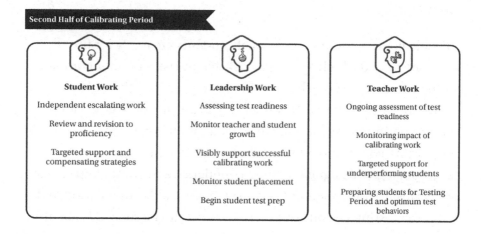

Second Half of Calibrating Period

Student Work

Independent escalating work

Review and revision to proficiency

Targeted support and compensating strategies

Leadership Work

Assessing test readiness

Monitor teacher and student growth

Visibly support successful calibrating work

Monitor student placement

Begin student test prep

Teacher Work

Ongoing assessment of test readiness

Monitoring impact of calibrating work

Targeted support for underperforming students

Preparing students for Testing Period and optimum test behaviors

By the end of the Calibrating Period, administrators and academic leaders need to start designing the optimal environment for the Testing Period and develop a test preparation plan to be rolled out and practiced at the end of this period. In a best practice situation, they would be visible in classrooms and supporting student effort and performance while marketing their vision for an effective testing situation.

Teachers and students need to contribute their thoughts on what an optimal environment might include. Discussions could involve:

- Physical conditions (e.g., lighting, room temperature, or room arrangement).
- Pre-and post-test activities and schedules.
- Students' preferred testing monitors.

Before testing begins, all environments, schedules, pre- and post-activities, and procedures need to be practiced and mastered. Academic leaders and teachers need to control identified distractors and have plans B and C ready for unanticipated crises or distractions.

In a best practice world, everything would run smoothly, but in the real world, plans must be flexible and adaptable to meet unforeseen situations.

All stakeholders should know which students are ready for the assessment and which are still at-risk. For at-risk students, compensating strategies need to be identified and practiced before the Calibrating Period ends. All students who are at-risk need an adult mentor during the second half of the Calibrating Period. They should meet with their mentor, discuss the factors that put them at-risk, and target strategies designed to build confidence and competence. Our goal is to have every student come out of the Calibrating Period and enter the Testing Period confident that they can be successful on the assessment.

Evaluating the Calibrating Period

Best Practice Indicators	Yes/No	Priority
Teachers developed and implemented tactical plans for increasing the levels of student performance to the levels expected on the state assessment.		
Teachers and coaches eliminated all ineffective teacher and student work and maximized effective time on-task.		
Lessons involved student work linking old learnings to assessments, new learnings to assessments, and real-world examples.		
Teachers provided calibrating activities and used that work to assess student readiness for the state test.		
Academic leaders lead PLC discussions of student assessment results in fine-tuned support systems for any student at-risk.		

Best Practice Indicators	Yes/No	Priority
All students had an opportunity to engage in the levels of work consistent with the levels of rigor and complexity found on the state assessment and received feedback on their performance and the opportunity to revise to proficiency.		
Academic leaders and coaches surveyed lesson plans to make sure that all power standards were covered completely in the Formative and Calibrating Periods.		
Students who consistently disrupted the learning or performing environment were assessed and a menu of alternative strategies was created.		
Academic leaders provided weekly feedback to all teachers on observed implementation and impact of tactical plans.		
In the month before the beginning of testing, academic leaders and PLC groups assessed school readiness and identified students who needed further assistance to reach their potential.		
In the month before the beginning of testing, academic leaders and coaches met with each teacher to establish plans for building optimal testing environments.		

Planning Next Year's Calibrating Period

Timeframe	Concerns/ Action Plan	Leader	Completion Date	Expected Outcome
By End of March				

07

THE TESTING PERIOD

Description: The Testing Period is not just the time when the test is administered to all students. It is the time when we build an optimal assessment environment, prepare the students for that environment, administer the test, and assess the success of our environment, enabling students to perform to their full potential.

Timeframe: The Testing Period begins two to three weeks before the test starts and lasts through the week following the test administration.

Goal: The goal of the Testing Period is to create an optimal assessment environment in which all students can and will demonstrate their potential as learner and performer.

Priorities for Academic Leaders:

- Market a vision for an optimal test environment to staff and students and provide opportunities for practice and scrimmage experiences.

- Practice revised test day schedules, rituals and routines, and student placements.

- Eliminate all extraneous distractions.

- Develop and market plans for predictable disruptions and for unexpected distractions and disruptions.

- Visibly support teachers and students in test preparation and testing best effort activities.

- Visit all classrooms to support teachers and students and to identify teachers and students who are out of sync with the testing plan.

- If problems are identified, meet daily with leadership team to form more plans - B and C.

- With leadership team, develop an end-of-year (EOY) plan.

- Interact with students individually to assess commitment and motivation and celebrate their effort and successes.

- Check all teachers' plans for debriefing and transition to EOY.

- Complete evaluations of the Opening Period, Formative Period, and Calibrating Period.

Priorities for Teachers:

- Plan test-taking rituals, routines, and schedules to ensure student mastery before the actual testing begins.

- Eliminate all extraneous distractions.

- Review effective test-taking strategies.

- Assess student mastery of test format and provide last-minute assistance.

- Maintain a focus on formative activities after the daily test is completed.

- Provide work to activate long-term memory.

- Plan to maintain learning momentum in the weeks before and after the test.

- Maintain an optimal classroom environment before, during, and after the test.

Priorities for Students:

- Attend school daily.

- Practice optimal preparation and test-taking rituals, routines, and schedules.

- Review and practice effective test-taking strategies.

- Highly engage in all test practice work and revise to proficiency.

- Self-assess test readiness and seek assistance if needed.

- Meet with adult mentor to discuss motivation and effort.

- Accept support when provided and actively engage in support activities.

In the week after the test, it's important for the entire staff to review the test preparation plan to evaluate the implementation and assess the impact on students. This is the beginning of planning for the next year and can help transition into the end of the year work to be done in the last period of the Learner Year.

Testing Period Self-Assessment – Overall School Readiness

Best Practice Indicators	Yes/No	Priority
Teachers and coaches have a plan for developing optimal testing environments in all classes.		
Academic leaders and coaches have developed backup plans for unforeseen disruption of the testing cycle (e.g., behavior, illness, emotional stress, etc.).		
Academic leaders, coaches, and instructional staff have established plans for mitigating all controllable disruptions (e.g., announcements, drills, maintenance, etc.).		
Student/teacher testing groups have been designed to match students with teachers who can solicit best-effort and high-level engagement for the course of the test.		
Administrators have planned for increased visibility before, during, and after testing and altered their observation checklists to meet the demands of the Testing Period.		
The school day during testing has been altered to ensure that all students can get to school, have breakfast, and go through pre-testing rituals.		
All teachers have been trained to engage students in pre-test focusing activities and post-test decompression activities.		
All teachers have plans to maintain the teaching/learning environment after the testing is completed for the day.		
All adult mentors and "lightning rods" have plans to meet daily with their target students to make sure they are emotionally ready for best-effort work on the test.		

TESTING PERIOD OVERVIEW

A turnaround school principal asked her Ed Directions' coach how important the Testing Period was in the overall scope of things. The coach answered that while the school focus should be on the EOY transition and on the competencies described in the standards, schools are held accountable for test scores and state labels. As educators, we are expected to build competent learners and performers and to prepare those students to make successful transitions to the next stage of their education or their lives. At the same time, we are expected to increase student performance on a paper and pencil test, and our status with the state's Department of Education will be defined (in part or in whole) by that test performance. Underperformance on the state assessment can have serious negative consequences for schools and for those staffs, and for this reason, we must take the test preparation part of our job seriously.

In many schools, the focus for planning the test is only on the administration. There are rules and regulations, ethical concerns, materials acquisition and distribution concerns, test coverage concerns, and behavior management concerns. These are all legitimate concerns. If we ignore any of them, we can cause many students to score below their potential. It is also possible, however, that we can do all of these things well and still allow students to underperform.

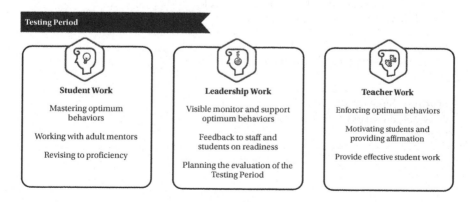

Testing Period

Student Work	Leadership Work	Teacher Work
Mastering optimum behaviors	Visible monitor and support optimum behaviors	Enforcing optimum behaviors
Working with adult mentors	Feedback to staff and students on readiness	Motivating students and providing affirmation
Revising to proficiency	Planning the evaluation of the Testing Period	Provide effective student work

Testing Period Self-Assessment – Leadership *Readiness*

Test Prep – Leadership	Covered in our Plan?	Priority
The school has planned for the academic, emotional, social, and physical environments.		
The test plan has been marketed and practiced by all stakeholders.		
School staff and students understand school and individual goals.		
Data-supported plan for testing and scheduling has been developed and practiced.		
All teachers understand the school plan for the Testing Period and have developed personal and class action plans to implement the school plan.		
Plans for administering the test - schedule, test administration, test exiting, and post-test activities - have been developed, tested, and adapted as needed.		
The school has practiced optimal test behaviors and all students understand expectations (e.g., 100 percent attendance, completing all tasks, etc.).		
Distractions have been systematically eliminated, and the school can maintain the two+-week schedule without major distractions.		
Every teacher has assessed his or her students and identified optimal environment requirements.		
Students have practiced and can maintain engagement and work from opening bell to closing bell.		

Test Prep – Leadership	Covered in our Plan?	Priority
Every teacher has *done the math* (see Doing the Math tool), regularly reviewed results, and communicated them to the principal.		
Teachers have assessed student needs and identified accommodating, compensating triage strategies that can help students reach their potential.		

Testing Period Readiness – Teacher Self-Assessment

Test Prep – Classrooms	Class Prepared?	Priority
All students understand non-cognitive factors that can reduce their performance and have a personal plan (e.g., an attendance plan) for remediating those factors.		
All "at-risk" or "must move" students have been assigned to cohort groups and have adult mentors with whom they discuss their progress regularly.		
All students have practiced and mastered the formats and venues of the state test.		
All students can develop rubrics for test questions and check answers against those rubrics.		
Students have been assigned to teachers that can address identified non-cognitive barriers (e.g., teacher dependence, attention deficit, or test anxiety for testing).		
Trial run experiences were provided for students to test their readiness and make personal plans.		
Students have established collective goals for the Testing Period and specific goals for each individual test.		

Test Prep – Classrooms	Class Prepared?	Priority
Data profiles and collections of student work from the Calibrating Period are used to monitor student growth and provide targeted assessment support.		
Ineffective teacher and student work were eliminated in the Calibrating Period.		
All students understand the test preparation plan and are motivated to give their best effort.		
All students understand the need for perfect attendance and timeliness and have practiced test week entry and exit protocols and schedules.		

In planning for the Testing Period, we must make our plans and build our environment from the student perspective first and then develop the adult components to enable all students to perform to their potential.

As in the other periods, there are specific things that we can develop to enable students to perform to their potential:

Competencies: In the Opening Period, we became focused on the competencies that students needed to be successful for the year. In the Formative Period, the focus was on building more proficient learners. In the Calibrating Period, it was on building more proficient performers. In the Testing Period, the focus is on building more effective test takers and preparing them to demonstrate proficiency. Competencies include format mastery, venue experience, test-taking strategies, individual triage strategies, and pre- and post-test taking strategies.

Conditioning for high-level assessments: High-level assessments require optimal environments, endurance conditioning, maintained high-level reading and thinking, and knowledge-based decision making. All of these requirements can be developed during the Testing Period. It is a disaster if a student knows the content but cannot maintain concentration, fails to endure the whole task or complete tasks, or is unable to maintain a level of performance through the entire Testing Period. Endurance is the key to maximum effort and best practice engagement.

5 Legged Model: Testing preparation involves the attitude, perception, thinking, and experience pieces of the 5 Legged Model. Students who have issues with attitude, perception, or thinking must get intensive and individualized attention in the Testing Period. Knowledge and experience can be developed in whole class work, but the other three legs need individual support on a daily basis.

Linking work: It is critical that students, especially students below high school, understand that learning and assessment are linked, and know that the types of questions that appear on assessments determine how they must be able to use what they have learned in class. Beginning about a month before the test, students need to get work regularly that links *what they are learning* to *test questions* and *the types of answers* they should produce on assessments.

The Opening Period and the Testing Period are the two shortest periods in the Learner Year. In both, we can make decisions that make life easier for the adults in the building but can miss our chance to have a significant impact on student scores on the state assessment. We have to understand that in these two periods, we are preparing the students for success. In the Opening Period, we equip them to be successful in class as learners and later as performers. In the Testing Period, we equip them to be successful test takers and to work to the level of their potential on a test. Both periods are necessary but not sufficient for making it possible for all students to reach their potential. However, both are critical to student success.

Making the wrong decisions or failing to meet student needs in these two periods undermines the chance we have to move all students. In the case of the Testing Period, failure to implement student-focused schedules, rituals, and routines — and to practice until students can follow them automatically — can cost the school its opportunity to reap benefits from the Formative and Calibrating Periods.

Planning a best practice assessment experience involves looking beyond just the content and academic strategies. These are important, but the emotional, testing, social, and physical testing environments are equally important. These areas are critical to optimizing student performance. Failure to address any can cause students who know the content — and can perhaps even do the work — to miss questions on an assessment.

Establishing an **appropriate academic environment** is, of course, critical to the test process. In many cases, schools address this with reviews and practice tests, but there's more to an academic environment than just review and practice.

Academic Leadership	Teachers	Students
Develop a consensus among all stake-holders about best practice test environments.	Build a performer-friendly class-room within the constraints of ethical expectations.	Commit to engage highly and give best effort.
Eliminate all controllable distractions and establish a protocol for dealing with ad hoc disturbances.	Introduce "brain-work" and focusing activities and practice for pre- and post-test transitions.	Commit to 100% attendance. Define tasks and complete all parts of tasks while working independently.
Establish entry/exit, pre-test, optimal behaviors, and sched-ules for the test week and practice until mastered.	Link prior learn-ings to assessments demonstrating how formats and venues can change with content.	Set and monitor goals for testing and for each individual test. Revise all work to proficiency.
Distribute students and match with teachers to create optimal rapport situations.	Provide shaping feed-back for all student work.	

A common barrier to optimal performance in students is the **emotional environment**. Emotional competency, defined as the ability to compartmentalize and stay focused, may not be in place in all students. Attending to emotional needs — personal needs or ad hoc situational needs — needs to be a part of test prep planning. Situational issues (e.g., an accident or emergency) can cause large numbers of students to underperform significantly, and personal issues (e.g., test anxiety or home issues) can cause individual students to perform well below potential. Planning to identify and deal with emotional issues can prevent a major loss of performance over a testing cycle.

Academic Leadership	Teachers	Students
Identify existing emotional issues and develop plans.

Anticipate possible issues and develop intervention and control plans.

Establish alternative schedules for testing to provide time to re-establish control and stability.

Eliminate negative interactions and stress-causing activities for the duration of the Testing Period. | Create a "we are in this together" atmosphere.

Identify students with specific emotional needs and begin developing compensating strategy plans.

Work with students to develop a plan for identifying emotional issues and getting support in place.

Celebrate student mastery of emotions, their efforts, and their successes. | Utilize an adult mentor to communicate emotional issues before they get in the way of performance.

Work with a peer group to support attendance and best effort.

Celebrate successes and effort with peer groups.

Develop compensating and control strategies to offset stress. |

Social issues can also cause students to underperform academically. The interactions between students and between students and teachers can create stress and cause distractions that disrupt momentum and cause loss of focus. Developing a vision for the way people will interact during the Testing Period is a critical piece of planning.

Academic Leadership	Teachers	Students
Design and market a mental model for the social environment (e.g., etiquette, rituals, and routines) that will provide stability for assessment.

Identify potential social issues (e.g., cliques, bullying, romances) that can create instability and cause academic or emotional issues.

Establish a practice schedule with feedback for the social environment and practice until mastered.

Distribute students and match with teachers to create optimal rapport situations. | Eliminate bullying and establish an etiquette for interaction between and among groups and individuals.

Identify potential social issues (e.g., romances) and immediately communicate problems to leadership.

Identify students exhibiting social issues and the link, if possible, to an adult for support.

Work with students to practice the etiquette, rituals, and routines that will be a part of the social environment. | Self-identify and seek support.

Work with a peer group to prepare and support.

Set personal goals and provide feedback to peers on their progress toward their goals.

Set and monitor goals for testing and for each individual test.

Practice alerting teachers to social issues that could result in reduced effort or performance. |

The physical environment of the building is a variable that can be difficult to control. If you have no air-conditioning, for example, you may have to deal with overheated classrooms. We must realize that the physical environment can have a significant impact on student performance. Anticipating problems in the physical environment and developing ad hoc plans is a part of test preparation that cannot be ignored.

Academic Leadership	Teachers	Students
Identify environmental issues — (e.g., heat — optimal range 72 to 82 degrees). Seek student input on how to improve the environment for the test (e.g., improve breakfast, placement of fans, or suggestions for bus routes). Manage the schedule and design breakfast and lunch menus and schedules to reflect best practices. Consider physical needs when distributing students and teachers for testing. Recognize student suggestions that are implemented and give students credit for being a part of the solution effort.	Control temperature and light if possible or, with the students, prepare for accommodation and compensation. Work with students to identify and deal with regular distractions and ad hoc situations. Communicate suggestions to administrators and recognize students when their suggestions are accepted. Eliminate distracting visuals and technologies. Consider gender needs for personal space when distributing students.	Assist in identifying and developing plans for physical environment issues. Assess personal needs in a physical environment and communicate those to the teachers. Help set up the room for best effort. Identify unforeseen problems and immediately communicate them to the teachers.

The test preparation portion of the Testing Period must be tightly planned to accomplish everything that leaders and teachers and students need to achieve before, during, and after the test. When we started working with test preparation, we focused on just the pre-test and Testing Periods. We found this didn't provide enough flexibility or enough time to do everything necessary to prepare and engage students for a high-level assessment.

For this reason, we now divide the Testing Period into four phases:

1. **Three to four weeks before the test starts, we enter *the prepa-ration phase.*** At this time, administrators, students, and teachers need to prepare the school and the students for the test. For the administrators, this means they must not only take care of the adult issues, they also need to find out how many barriers to student success create serious issues and begin planning to prepare both students and school staff to help students overcome those barriers. Teachers need to provide work that links new and old learnings to sample test questions and to standards expectations. Students need to practice optimal behaviors (e.g., getting to school, completing tasks, etc.) and contribute high-level engagement of work to prepare them to demonstrate their potential on a high-stakes assessment. It is also important during this phase of the Testing Period to address attitude and perception issues and link "must move" students to an adult who has access to those students.

Focus	Leadership	Teachers	Students
Get the school the staff and the students ready for an optimal assessment experience.	Finalize the assessment plan and market the plan to staff and students. Anticipate possible interruptions or disruptions and have intervention plans in place. Identify at-risk students and initiate personal contact. Eliminate all adult and student distractions. Buffer staff and students from extraneous stress. Monitor cohort groups for implementation and impact.	Introduce the classroom assessment culture and begin practicing rituals, routines, and etiquette. Link assessment models to prior learnings. Introduce "test wise" strategies. Assist students in setting set short-term and Testing Period goals. Emphasize optimal behavior expectations. Practice compensation strategies.	Have perfect attendance. Demonstrate high levels of engagement and effort. Establish personal goals for assessment. Practice etiquette and optimal behaviors. Relate diversified learning and performing needs to the assessment format and venue. Establish "personal best" portfolio of assessment answers. Celebrate successes.

2. **The week before the test is *the activating phase.*** During this week, we practice the schedule, rituals, and routines that we plan to use during the test week and provide feedback on student perception of the schedule, rituals, and routines. Administrators need to be visible in classrooms, supporting student effort. Recognitions of success in the schedules, rituals, and routines need to be celebrated and encouraged during this week. The

"must move" students need daily contact with their adult mentor, and all students who have been trained to use triage strategies need to have those strategies reviewed and utilized. Personal contact with academic leaders — especially proactive, motivating contact — can help motivate and focus students.

Focus	Leadership	Teachers	Students
Provide real-time development and rehearsal for assessment.	Visible support with monitoring of test preparation. Motivate target students. Field-test the master test schedule, the optimal behaviors, and the test etiquette. Plan student-teacher groupings to elicit optimal effort and support.	Practice and provide dress rehearsals for etiquette, assessment rituals and routines, and test schedules. Provide long-term memory work. Set short-term and Testing Period goals. Practice compensation strategies.	Have perfect attendance. Demonstrate high levels of engagement and effort. Monitor personal goals. Mastery of etiquette and optimal behaviors. Mastery of compensating strategies.

3. **The third phase of the Testing Period is *the test itself*.** Administrators and teachers need to have a "we are ready for this" attitude as students enter the building each day and need to recognize the students' efforts as they leave the building. Students need to be reminded daily of the way the day's schedule will operate and encouraged to "show them what we can do." Each day, teachers and students need to review the next day's assessment and what students have done to get ready.

4. **The week after the test is *a refocusing and transition phase*.**
    It's a time when we can debrief with the students and honor their
    effort and successes and help them prepare for the type of work
    that the class will do for the rest of the year. We emphasize that
    the goal for this work is to help all students make a successful
    transition to next year.

Focus	Leadership	Teachers	Students
Recognize and celebrate the effort and the success of the assessment plan. Transition to the EOY activities.	Market an EOY plan and check teacher tactical plans. Emphasize that the year is not over. Evaluate the test preparation and plan to determine priorities for next year. Begin developing the strategic plan for opening school next year.	Affirm work and effort observed during the test. Identify the learning goals for the EOY. Begin transition activities. Begin developing plans for students during the summer.	Have perfect attendance. Demonstrate continued high-level engagement. Initial inventory of summer interests and opportunities. Introduction to the next year's program and expectations. Complete capstone or collective activities.

We emphasize that there is no time in the Testing Period for ineffective teacher or student work. Any ineffective work during this
period will not just cause a learning problem but will cause students
to underperform on the test itself. There are some types of student
work that have been identified as effective in all phases of test
prep planning.

TESTING PERIOD – EFFECTIVE PRACTICES FOR STUDENT WORK

Effective work in the Testing Period may include effective learning and calibrating work that needs to expand the student work experience. Students need to be highly engaged in activities that prepare them to use learnings in a variety of assessment situations.

Directed Strategy	Definition	Impact on Student Potential
Linking Work	Linking work provides students with an opportunity to examine their classwork and identify, in terms of testing and standards, expectations of why they are doing that work.	Linking work validates the work students do in class and makes it more meaningful in terms of their learning. If used regularly, it also builds access to long-term memory centers and provides opportunities to use information from long-term memory to answer questions and solve problems. It also gives the teachers a chance to link critical reading and thinking, and purposeful writing to both the learning and performing processes.
Focusing Work	Focusing work is student work experience that expands the students' ability to focus on the work at hand and stay engaged over time. Many teachers use centering work for initial relaxation and focus followed by focusing strategies that enable the students to get engaged and stay engaged in work.	Focus is a critical issue for younger students. Getting focused, maintaining focus, and staying engaged in lengthy tasks is required on state assessments. However, attention and prioritizing issues can cause younger students to become distracted, lose focus, and lose the integrity of their thinking and answering process. Focusing work and focusing strategies provide an adult strategy set for students who are not yet adults, and these strategies can enable them to perform beyond their maturation level.

Directed Strategy	Definition	Impact on Student Potential
Test Wiseness Work	Test wiseness work is essential; however, test preparation is still a bad word in some districts. And yet students, especially students below tenth grade, can struggle when they are in unfamiliar settings. If the format, the venue, or the duration pulls them out of their comfort zone, they can perform well below their potential and miss questions when they know the content. Teaching the students to attack tests intentionally and with strategies can build their confidence, encourage them to take risks, and eliminate format, venue, and duration as potential disqualifiers.	Students who have test strategies in hand are more apt to overcome test anxiety, approach unfamiliar test items with confidence, take risks in generating an answer, and have an accurate view of their performance on an assessment. Students with test wiseness will frequently outscore students who own more content but go into the test cold, relying on memory to carry them through the assessment.

Directed Strategy	Definition	Impact on Student Potential
Task Analysis	Task analysis is a type of work that was used extensively in the 1980s and early 1990s. In this work, identifying the task(s) required for proficiency was half of the assignment. Students first identified what they had to do, then developed a plan to make sure all of the work was done and completed. The research that led to this work was fundamental to the development of the four-column method. Students who can task analyze are more intentional test takers and miss fewer questions because they make an impulsive but incorrect response. This impulsiveness is one of the characteristics of students until well into the high school curricula. Developing a thinking ritual to identify the tasks that are actually being asked for causes students to be more intentional and more effective test takers.	Impulsivity is a major problem with immature students. Giving them an adult thinking strategy — identify what it is you have to do — makes them more thoughtful and more accurate test takers. They are more likely to use embedded clues or prompts, identify the real answer required for a test, and exhibit confidence when they know at least some of the content or task set required by the question.

During the Testing Period, we look for different types of work in each phase of the period. Linking work and task analysis work are critical in the preparation phase. In the activating phase, focusing work takes priority. The debriefing and transitioning work become priorities in the post-test period.

Step 1: Introduction to a strategy or approach with teacher modeling and collective use.

Step 2: Student use with direction or alerts provided by the teacher.

Step 3: Student use in collaborative peer-group monitoring.

Step 4: Peer-group feedback and rubric-based shaping feedback.

Step 5: Independent use with teacher monitoring, peer-group feedback, and rubric-based shaping feedback.

Step 6: Independent use with rubric-based self-assessment and revision to proficiency with peer review on proficiency.

Step 7: Independent identification of critical learnings and independent development of personalized strategies.

TESTING PERIOD – INEFFECTIVE PRACTICES FOR STUDENT WORK

Ineffective Work	What It is	Impact on Students
Purposeless work.	Work that is not perceived as valuable by students. They do not relate to what they need to learn or what they are expected to do.	Purposeless work is deadly in the Testing Period. During test preparation, all work must have a test-relevant purpose or students can lose focus and momentum which are critical for maintaining high levels of engagement and endurance on a lengthy, complex test.
Work that is at an inappropriate level or uses an inappropriate format.	Off-level work and formats are frequently used for students who are perceived to be off-level to "help them" be successful.	Off-level work and formats cause students to develop self-perceptions, work habits, and comfort zones that will prevent them from working at the levels required by an assessment. Off-level work will almost guarantee that students will perform below their potential.
Fun stuff.	Teachers are frequently reluctant to introduce new learnings just before, during, and just after the test. Many times, they look for activities that are relaxing and/or fun.	These activities absorb time and often engage the students, but they do not move the students toward success. Many times, they distract the students from the business at hand, which is reaching their potential on the test. The cost in losing focus, losing time, and producing ineffective work product can be significant.

Ineffective Work	What It is	Impact on Students
Assessments that include formats and venues that are not a part of the expected standards.	Test "prep" that includes formats or venues that are not in test specifications.	It is critical that students master all the formats, genres, and venues they will face on state or national assessments. Without this practice, they can know content, but because they aren't fluent with answering the different types of questions, working in a venue, or working for as long as the question may require, they can miss the question. This gives a false read of student performance and, depending on the number of students involved, can have a major impact on the overall school score.

Ineffective student work can be seriously detrimental to student performance on the assessment. Work that distracts students or undermines optimal rituals and routines can break the focus of students — especially students who are at-risk — and can cause the students to perform below their potential. This gives us a false read of what actually happened with those students during the year, and also reinforces problems with attitudes, perceptions, and work ethics the teachers have spent most of the school year trying to remediate. Administrators need to carefully monitor the work students are doing outside the test timeframe to make sure it doesn't undo the good work done during the rest of the year and set the stage for failure in the next phase of the test.

It is important that teacher work support optimal student performance. Some teacher practices that were effective in the Formative and Calibrating Periods can be detrimental in the Testing Period. For example, in the Formative and Calibrating Periods, teachers used period-specific directed activities and guided practice to prepare the students for success. Using these strategies during the Testing Period can reaffirm teacher dependence in students who are insecure or who have become teacher-dependent in the course of their education. Administrators need to be aware of effective and ineffective teacher work patterns and strategies.

TESTING PERIOD – EFFECTIVE STRATEGIES FOR TEACHERS

Work Pattern	Definition	Samples
Create optimal assessment classrooms.	Literate classrooms include supportive visuals, multiple genres related to the content taught, and a variety of equipment and technology related to expanding student understanding.	Cross-discipline, cumulative, capstone, and flow-chart visuals. Computers and other technologies that provide alternative sources of data for students to acquire and interpret. A variety of different written or graphic materials that students can use to enhance learning or understanding.
Make the class a learning lab.	Students and teachers should be a teaching/learning team. Experimenting with testing environments, take risks, and reverse roles to enhance teaching and learning.	Student-developed rubrics. Student-developed test questions or student analysis of test questions and responses.

Work Pattern	Definition	Samples
Provide an optimal learning environment.	As in the Calibrating Period, it's important that learning work goes bell-to-bell. There will not be enough time to do everything that has to be done if there are adult or student interruptions that break the momentum of the lesson or the rhythm of the learning.	Effective academic and behavior rituals and routines that are enforced consistently and fairly. Fine-tuning classroom arrangements and student placements in classes. Realigning student/teacher assignments to provide a better match.
Preparing quizzes and assessments utilizing the venue, format, and duration expectations of the class for state assessments.	Preparing students for different formats, venues, and levels is an important preparation piece. As in the Calibrating Period, identifying how the same content can be tested at third, eighth, and tenth grades can be a very effective way to introduce levels to students. Similarly, selecting different types of multiple-choice questions, short-answer questions, or open-response questions can prepare students to attack those questions with confidence. By the time students take the test, they should have successfully answered every type of question they will face on the test.	Introduction to the different types of questions. Providing questions in advance and having the students link their learning to the question. Giving a grade for using a testing strategy as well as for an answer. Making a part of the grade the correct identification of the type of question. Having students develop different types of questions as an activity or an assessment of learning. Providing multiple levels of the same question so the students can "challenge up" from where they think they are to the next level of question.

In one school, an advanced program teacher threw a temper tantrum over "time lost" for a state test. The negative attitude carried over to the students, and the school's score dropped considerably because nearly all of the advanced program students underperformed.

In one school, an advanced program teacher threw a temper tantrum over "time lost" for a state test. The negative attitude carried over to the students, and the school's score dropped considerably because nearly all of the advanced program students underperformed.

As with students, teachers can also engage in ineffective practices. These practices can distract the students, break their concentration, reinforce problems with perception of self or attitudes about school, and redirect student thinking to venues other than school and tests. For the most part, ineffective teacher practice relates to those student work patterns that were identified in the "ineffective student work" materials above. It's important for leaders to do an attitude check on all staff to make sure that everybody is onboard with the school plan. Negative input from teachers — especially respected teachers — can undermine all of the work done during the year.

TESTING PERIOD – PLANNING/ EVALUATING WORKSHEET

Testing Period Best Practice	Priority for Next Year
The school developed a plan for the Testing Period that identified leadership, teacher, and student priorities.	
The school plan was translated by all staff into personal action plans, and leadership developed a shared sense of urgency and 100 percent buy-in for the test preparation plan.	
Students and teachers were redistributed to obtain optimal learning and performance from all students.	
School leaders and coaches monitored student work closely in the periods preceding the test and met regularly to deal with issues identified.	
Critical elements of the school plan were practiced during the month before the test to ensure consensus implementation.	
Plans included strategies to control and optimize the physical, academic, and emotional environments to optimize performance.	
Data was collected on pre-test, testing, and post-test implementation and impact on students, teachers, grade levels, and student cohort groups.	
Physical environment issues were controlled, and the physical environment of all test areas fell within the optimal range.	
Controllable distractions were eliminated, and plans enabled the school to reduce the impact of ad hoc distractions.	
Social and emotional issues were dealt with in a timely manner, and no classes or individual students suffered because of social or emotional issues that went unresolved.	

Testing Period Best Practice	Priority for Next Year
The leadership team met daily to assess implementation and impact and develop ad hoc plans for significant issue areas.	
The testing plan includes rituals and routines that have been practiced by all leaders, teachers, and students.	
The implementation and impact of critical activities were analyzed daily to assess the effect/goal relationship.	
Leadership, coaches, and "lightning rod" teachers met daily with their target students to encourage, motivate, and support.	
During the Testing Period, schedules were modified to enable teachers and coaches to address significant student performance concerns.	
Attendance, student distribution, and scheduling plans were implemented by all staff and achieved their desired results.	
Our final estimates of individual student performance, specific cell scores, and final school grades were very close to our actual scores.	
The testing plan provides for a smooth transition to EOY activities for all staff and students.	

Including students in the evaluation of the Testing Period can be beneficial in several ways:

- It gives administrators a student's eye view of how testing went and what they think could be done better.

- It can also help shape student attitudes and perceptions about their access to decision-making in the school.

- This can change attitude and perception and reinforce the idea that the school's culture is student focused.

- This can also stimulate discussions between teachers and students about what optimal test conditions are and why teachers and administrators look for certain optimal behaviors during test week.

In one school, the Ed Directions coach and the principal decided that these discussions would involve students with the teachers they would probably have next year to help begin the transition from one year to the next. It also set up the EOY activities that the principal and Ed Directions wanted to make sure happened before students left for the summer.

Planning for Next Year's Testing Period

Timeframe	Concerns/ Action Plan	Leader	Completion Date	Expected Outcome
By the End of April				

"However beautiful the strategy, you should occasionally look at the results."

– Winston Churchill

08

THE END-OF-YEAR PERIOD

Description: The End-of-Year (EOY) Period moves the students from the state Testing Period through the last day of school. In best practice, it is a time to achieve closure and to begin transition and best practice work for all stakeholders. We sometimes think of this as the beginning of the next school year.

Timeframe: The EOY begins two weeks after testing concludes and ends on the last day of school.

Goals: The goals for the EOY include:

- Bringing the current year's learning to a close.
- Doing work that helps organize all of this year's learnings in long-term memory.
- Transition activities to help the students move into an effective summer experience and make a successful transition to the next level.
- Aggregating the current year's data for summer planning.

Priorities for Academic Leaders:

- Develop and market an EOY plan with the leadership team and teaching staff.
- Celebrate their EOY effort and successes.
- Check and monitor all teachers' plans for transition to EOY.
- Complete an evaluation of the Opening, Formative, Calibrating, and Testing Periods.
- Begin planning for next year's SIP.

Priorities for Teachers:

- Maintain learning momentum through the last day of school.
- Bring closure to teaching and learning for the year.
- Enable a successful transition to the next grade level or the next stage.
- Celebrate the learning, hard work, and successes of the year.
- With students, plan summer activities that maintain performance, build language, and extend experience.
- Collect final data points and final student profiles.

Priorities for Students:

- Attend school daily.
- Stay engaged until the last day of school.
- Continue meeting with adult mentors to plan summer activities.

End-of-Year Readiness Self-Assessment

Best Practice Indicators	Yes/No	Priority
Academic leaders, teachers, and students celebrated the hard work and effort that went into the testing and jointly planned the EOY transition.		
Teachers worked with academic leaders and coaches to develop effective EOY experiences that would help students maintain learning over the summer and make a successful transition to the next year.		
Staff has started updating student profiles so that an EOY profile can be completed and passed on to next year's teachers.		
Academic leaders and coaches have worked with PLC groups to assess each period of the Learner Year and started redesigning next year's program.		
Teachers have reflected on their performance over the Learner Year and have identified professional development experiences they feel will make them more confident and competent as leaders of learners.		
Academic leaders and coaches have identified professional development experiences that will increase their confidence and competence as academic leaders.		
The school has a plan for the EOY to ensure teaching and learning continue until the end, students are engaged in quality work, dismissal can be conducted safely and orderly, and have a positive attitude about the summer and next year.		
Teachers and students have been assessed to identify interests, talents, and needs that can be addressed in summer programs and a menu of adult and student activities has been created.		
Academic leaders, coaches, and teachers have planned an EOY activity to celebrate success and begin planning for next year.		
Academic leaders have created observation checklists to be used in monitoring the implementation and impact of the EOY tactical plans.		

THE END-OF-YEAR PERIOD OVERVIEW

In many schools, the End-of-Year Period is wasted time. This could be because testing came so late in the year that there isn't enough time to do major learning worker development, but with planning, there are best practices that can extend student learning and prepare successful transitions. Even with limited time available, it is possible to provide students with work experiences that:

- Build long-term memory links.

- Bring learning and student work to closure.

- Enable students to take ownership over their learning, their work, and their success.

- Prepare students to engage in meaningful work over the summer and make a successful transition to the next year.

By the time the Testing Period closes, academic leaders should have marketed an EOY plan, and the teachers should have created personal action plans for the last weeks of school.

The final period of the school year involves reflection, self-assessment, and planning for all stakeholders. Teachers and administrators must assess this year's successes, identify areas of growth, and begin strategic planning for next year. For teachers and administrators, it is important to bring closure to their work and to begin the new work cycle for next year. The key to success in this effort will be the collection and organization of data on leadership, teachers, and students.

For students, the last period of the year is usually a fadeout into the summer. However, educators have the opportunity to do some things with students that are beneficial to building their capacity as self-initiated learners, preparing them to take ownership of their performance and make a successful transition into their next year.

If teachers aren't prepared to design and monitor effective EOY work, ad hoc professional development may need to be offered and coaching support provided.

In general, there are two types of best-practice work for students in the EOY Period. The first brings closure to this year and helps the students organize what they've learned into long-term memory. The second begins the students' successful transition from one year to the next Learner Year. It can introduce them to the content expectations, rituals and routines, and learning work expectations of the next year. In schools with stable teacher populations, students can be introduced to and work with the teachers they will have in the next year.

EOY Student Work	*Definition*	*Examples*
Closure or Capstone Activity	An EOY process that allows students to independently or in groups recall and use learnings in a long-term project. Any program that establishes an endpoint for a learning set and links the learnings to prior learnings or an assessment.	• A multi-grade study that is summarized each year using the learnings of that year (e.g., "What we've learned this year that can help make our community better."). • Create a glossary for each subject area at a grade level to present to incoming students or store in a classroom literacy center.

EOY Student Work	Definition	Examples
Transition/ Bridging	An activity that enables a successful transition from one grade, program, or level to another.	• Orientation programs (e.g., seventh graders visit sixth grade classrooms to talk with them about what to expect in seventh grade, or class visits to the next school the students will attend to observe classes and teachers). • Teacher exchange programs (e.g., seventh grade teachers teach the last sixth grade unit to introduce seventh grade work and content).
Access Analysis	A student analysis of personal access patterns (e.g., to teachers, other students, etc.).	• Student self-assessment activity (e.g., students identify teachers they could talk to and teachers they avoided). • Students list school leaders that they talked to outside of class. • Students develop a profile of the teacher they like best and the teacher they learned the most from as a portfolio entry.
Personal Summer Action Plan	An activity that establishes a personal commitment to do something to become a better student/ learner over the summer. Any activity that identifies student interests or enthusiasms.	• Build a personal reading list. • Identify interests, talents, or hobbies that can be pursued over the summer. • Identify "immersion learning" opportunities of interest. • Identify experience-widening opportunities.

EOY Student Work	Definition	Examples
Formative Work with Engagement	Quality work that introduces students to the formative work of the next year, possibly with the teacher(s) the students will have the next year.	• Introduction activity (e.g., sixth grade students demonstrate to their seventh-grade teachers how they learn best). • Seventh grade teachers give examples of seventh grade content in a model unit.
Team Building	An activity (e.g., shared ordeal, adventure, or interest activity) with next year's teachers and peers.	• A mini-field trip that takes students out of their comfort zone. • An activity that enables students and teachers to learn together. • A challenge activity where teachers and students share expertise.
EOY Parent Program	An activity or program that allows teachers and students to show parents what they've learned and what they've learned to do.	• Parent introduction to state assessments, having students explain to parents how to answer the questions. • Student recognition night where students share with parents their portfolio of work from the year.
Self-study/Introduction	An activity that enables student to reflect on self and prepare an introduction to next year's teachers.	• Student development of an introduction presentation to next year's teachers including "How I learn best and what I want to be." • Collecting an introductory portfolio of a student's best work from last year to present to next year's teachers.

EOY Student Work	Definition	Examples
Support Service Identification	An activity that alerts students to summer support, extension, or enrichment opportunities and encourages participation.	• Identify support programs offered by the school or community that address personal academic needs. • Establish a "growth checklist" or summer work schedule designed to build learner or performer strengths.
"Personal Best" Analysis	An activity that encourages student analysis of the year's work with a portfolio of "best work" samples from courses or programs.	• Build a portfolio of "best work" as learner, as performer, or as artist to be shared with parents or the next year's teacher. • Students identify the unit where they learned the most or the unit where the teacher did the best job of teaching and include an explanation of why.

The most important thing about the EOY is that students see the period work as academically important. The weeks or days left in the school year after the state test shouldn't be wasted. There are valuable types of student work that can be included that can continue the work of building the student as learner and performer.

Teachers also need to bring closure to their year, and this needs to involve work beyond emptying the trash can and locking the door. An important task is to do assessments of self and of the students that were in class this year.

One form of self-assessment is an EOY unit review:

Unit #	Subject or Focus	Duration and Number of Lessons	Number of Students Passing the Unit Test	Rank Order from Most Effective to Least	Notes for Improvement

Another form of self-assessment involves analysis of self as teacher/leader of learners:

Area	Rating
Preparation – classroom, curriculum, materials.	☐ Effective ☐ Adequate ☐ Growth area
Opening school.	☐ Effective ☐ Adequate ☐ Growth area
Establishing behavior rituals and routines.	☐ Effective ☐ Adequate ☐ Growth area
Establishing academic rituals and routines.	☐ Effective ☐ Adequate ☐ Growth area
Developed effective student formative work, eliminated all ineffective work, and supported all students' growth as learners.	☐ Effective ☐ Adequate ☐ Growth area
Developed differentiating learning work and performing work and addressed students' needs.	☐ Effective ☐ Adequate ☐ Growth area
Effective calibrating work, eliminated all ineffective work, and supported all students' development of performance competencies.	☐ Effective ☐ Adequate ☐ Growth area
Created an optimal testing environment that enabled all students to reach their potential and encouraged proficiency.	☐ Effective ☐ Adequate ☐ Growth area
Maintained optimum behavior and high levels of engagement.	☐ Effective ☐ Adequate ☐ Growth area

Area	Rating
Provided an end-of-year experience for students that brought closure to this year's learnings and prepared the students to engage in summer activities and make a successful transition to the next level.	☐ Effective ☐ Adequate ☐ Growth area
Used available student data and the self-analysis worksheets to develop a summer growth plan.	☐ Effective ☐ Adequate ☐ Growth area

Another area that teachers need to complete to bring to closure at the end of the year is a development of a student profile, as shown "EOY Student Profile" on page 242. This profile will give teachers information about the students they will have next year so they can begin planning. In the Ed Directions toolkit, coaches have a number of tools that can be used to describe students along with tools that enable students to describe themselves and how they learn and perform.

This profile development can be not only a tool for labeling and sorting students, but also a best practice activity because:

- It gives teachers a preliminary look at student successes and failures, strengths and concerns, and prior academic success.

- It can identify how students feel they learn best and under what conditions they perform best.

- It identifies possible problems, at-risk students, and previous teacher evaluations of student strengths and weaknesses.

- It captures cognitive and noncognitive data on all five legs of the performance model.

- Most importantly, it gives the teacher an opportunity to assess their readiness to teach these kids.

EOY Student Profile

Student _____ Grade _____ Year _____ Teacher _____

Non-Cognitive Data

Age: _____

Days Absent: _____

Tardies to School: _____

Tardies to Class: _____

Discipline Referrals: _____

Cause/Place:

Parent Conferences: _____

Reason(s):

Extra-Curricular Involvement:

Physical or Mental Issues:

Emotional Issues:

Special Talents or Interests:

Academic Data

Grades:

Reading/Language Arts _____

Math _____

Science _____

Social Studies _____

Art _____

Music _____

Health/PE _____

Other _____

Experiences:

Books Read _____

Words/Minute _____

Performance(s)/ Involvement:

Best Performance:

Best Class (Worst Class):

Assessment Data Points

Date	Test	Score
1.		
2.		
3.		
4.		
5.		
6.		
7.		
8.		
9.		
10.		

State Assessment Performance

Test	Expected Score	Actual Score
Reading		
Writing		
Math		
Science		

Notes

Access Adult(s):

Other:

Positive

Characteristic	Yes	Notes
Independent		
Attentive		
Long-term memory		
Critical vocabulary		
Format master		
Critical reading		
Critical thinking		
Critical writing		
Operational vocabulary		
Experience		
Good attitude		
Good work ethic		
Perception		
Revises work		
Supportive home		
High expectations		
Positive peer group		

What worked:

Concern

Characteristic	Yes	Notes
Attitude problem		
Attention problem		
Work ethic problem		
Informal language		
Endurance problem		
Little home support		
Impulsive		
Behavior problem		
Low expectations		
Little language experience		
Low self-esteem		
Negative peer group		
Attendance problem		
Easily led astray		
Demands attention		
Physical or mental issue		

Notes:

Do they have the skills to address behavior issues? Can they motivate students? Will their favorite lessons work for the students? Will they need other differentiation strategies? When academic leaders begin working with teachers on next year's school improvement plans, these questions need to drive the professional development and material selection plans for the year.

For instructional leaders and school administrators, there are several EOY compliance and regulatory activities that take up enormous amounts of time. There may be a temptation to focus only on those since they have legal and district policy implications. They are important, but transitioning effectively into the next year's learner cycle is a critical concern.

Evaluating the End-of-Year Period

Best Practice Indicators	Yes/No	Priority
All teachers developed and implemented effective EOY activities.		
Academic leaders and coaches were visible in classrooms and hallways, participating in the EOY activities and encouraging students.		
Adult mentors and "lightning rods" monitored their students through the last dismissal and saw them off with a positive message for next year.		
Academic leaders, coaches, and teachers worked with students to select EOY activities that matched interests, talents, or needs.		
Students stayed engaged in work until the last day of class.		

Best Practice Indicators	Yes/No	Priority
Academic leaders and coaches met with teachers, attended PLC discussions, developed a list of successful plans that need to be continued, and identified priority concerns that need to be addressed in the SIP and staff tactical plans.		
Academic leaders conferenced with teachers over perceived needs for professional development and developed individual professional development plans.		
Final student profiles were collected and studied to determine identified at-risk characteristics or behaviors.		
Academic leaders and teachers met in PLC groups to evaluate the EOY plan and developed suggestions for next year's SIP.		

Planning Next Year's EOY Period

Time-frame	Concerns/ Action Plan	Leader	Completion Date	Expected Outcome
By June 1				

09

BONUS SUMMER PERIOD (YEAR TWO)

THE SUMMER PERIOD (AFTER THE FIRST YEAR'S EXPERIENCE WITH THE RHYTHM OF THE LEARNER YEAR)

Description: The Bonus Summer Period (Summer Two) combines everything from a leader's first Summer Period (mostly focused on systems, facilities, and planning) and adds new layers of data collection, teacher evaluation, causal analysis of student performance, and more in-depth planning for opening school.

Once leadership has been through an entire cycle of the Learner Year, causal data, planning, and monitoring become critical to continued success. Leadership must both continue to expand the depth of knowledge of the current teachers as well as prepare for how to onboard new faculty and support staff. As this process is understood and institutionalized at a school, leadership can push more of the planning and accountability down to academic coaches, teachers, and, in terms of progress monitoring and self-assessment, the students. This second Summer Period chapter has more tools and strategies.

Timeframe: Like the first Summer Period, Summer Two is divided into two sub-periods. The first sub-period (first half of summer) is devoted to an analysis of what did and didn't work the previous year. This period begins with the end of the student year and lasts three to four weeks into the summer.

The second sub-period (the second half of summer) focuses on preparing the facility and staff for the students who are going to show up on the first day of school. This period begins when the evaluation of the previous year is completed and lasts until the Opening Period begins — about two to three weeks before the students arrive.

Goals: After the first year of working with the Rhythm of the Learner Year, the focus continues on the development of school capacity to move students. Use both periods of the summer for best practice activities for the administrative team, teaching, and support staff and the students themselves. The largest difference between Summer One and Summer Two is that leadership is using a much larger and more targeted data set as well as a year of practical knowledge of planning based on student work and teaching the whole child with the 5 Legged Model.

The facilities and operational readiness are still high priorities. Closing out year one and preparing for year two can be much more nuanced in curricula planning, professional development, data collection planning, and onboarding new faculty and support staff. Everyone plays his or her part in supporting the leadership's plans and goals.

Priorities for Academic Leaders:

- Complete an in-depth analysis of each academic year period to determine the extent to which the school plan was implemented and the impact of that implementation on student performance.

- Provide training and developmental experience for academic leaders to move them from awareness and practitioner level to mastery level.

- Provide training for teachers and support staff to move from awareness level to at least practitioner level and target some for a leadership development experience set.

- Provide a menu of student activities that can expand student language or experience base, maintain performance levels, or build life experience for students who have limited experience.

- Provide programs that build access to decision making for all staff and help build both top-down and bottom-up access to problem-solving and decision-making.

- Develop a strategic plan that can be turned into tactical plans by all staff.

- Plan for an opening of school that includes best practice opportunities for students and staff to start the year successfully.

- Sort and place students to create effective teaching and learning teams.

- Get the facilities, materials, and technologies in efficient working order.

- Plan and provide orientation programs for all new parents and staff and for all students with their new teachers.
- Evaluate and upgrade management and academic systems.
- Provide the ad hoc PD needed to prepare staff to lead learners and learning teams.
- Review the evaluation of the Opening, Formative, Calibrating, Testing, and EOY Periods. Identify needed changes and begin prioritizing for SIP.

Priorities for Teachers:

- Evaluate the year, identifying successes and failures, and revise plans.
- Plan summer activities and growth opportunities.
- Collect student profiles and begin identifying "at-risk" students.
- Plan the rituals and routines, orientation, and initial learning activities for next year's opening.
- Develop a scaffold for next year's units, establish learning goals for each unit, and prepare the formative student work for the first work units.
- Collect final data points and final student profile student metadata.

Priorities for Students:

- Read at least 30 minutes every day.
- Complete all summer maintenance work provided by teachers.
- Participate in immersion and growth activities offered by the school or community.
- Participate in school orientation and transition activities at the end of the summer.

After the first year of working with the Rhythm of the Learner Year, it's possible to develop a much more effective and efficient plan for summer activities. Most of the academic leaders and teachers will have moved from the awareness level to at least the practitioner level and might be ready to move on to the mastery level. Students and staff will have had a year's experience working with effective student work and formative student assessments. For teachers, this refers to the design and engagement of students in the work and assessments. For students, it relates to learning and being highly engaged in assigned work and completing all tasks: developing the habits of mind, attitudes, and perceptions that support effective learning.

Are We Ready for the Summer Period?

Best Practice Indicators	Yes/No	Priority
Have we evaluated our performance during each period of the Learner Year and developed plans for the next school year?		
Did we develop EOY profiles on all of our students with recommendations for placement and support next year?		
Have we identified areas within our academic and management systems that need to be evaluated and updated?		
Have we evaluated the staff that will be returning to the school next year, targeted some for leadership development and others for summer assistance, and facilitated planning?		
Do we have a plan for academic leaders, teachers, support staff, and students that will prepare them for greater success next year?		
Have we begun the development of an SIP and secured the human and financial resources, the materials, and the time that we will need to turn the SIP into tactical plans, monitor the implementation and impact of the plan, and revise the plan as needed?		

When Ed Directions' coaches work with a school to plan the summer after their first year implementing the Rhythm of the Learner Year, they usually start by focusing on the student. If the student isn't kept in the equation, it's easy for the adults to lapse back into their adult-focused planning patterns.

THE "STUDENTS IN THE SUMMER" CONUNDRUM

Many years ago, when the authors of this book were students, there was very little that happened during the summer that related to school. Some of us read books, but for the most part, we did not engage in learning activities. Talented students might pursue music or art lessons, and very few might get involved in theater, but for the most part, school didn't enter the picture. This was unfortunate because there are many opportunities for students during the summer that are important for learning and performing:

- **Immersion Programs:** These programs allow students to engage in "deep learning" in a subject that the student finds interesting. This type of experience changes the learner for life and causes the student to become a self-actualized learner, which is a key to lifelong learning and independent thinking. It also improves the way the brain works and makes it possible for the student to be a much more efficient learner and performer.

- **Capstone Programs:** These programs engage learners in an activity that causes them to use all of their learnings from the previous year to perform a task. Often this is connected to community study or community improvement activities, but it can also involve portfolio development or survival guides for next year's students taking the class. Capstone activities, like immersion activities, involve students in "deep" use of learning in real-world situations. This changes the way the brain works and creates multiple cueing passes for independent retrieval of learnings later.

- **Community Service Programs:** Community service activities enable students to learn about real-world connections between school and community by doing something to improve the quality of life for the school or the greater community. Community service programs build real-world vocabulary and provide an opportunity for real-world uses of reading, mathematics, and critical thinking. They are also instrumental in developing planning skills and leadership potential.

- **Maintenance or Remediation Programs:** For the past several decades, educators have been studying the problem of performance loss over the summer. Loss begins after two weeks out of school and increases through the summer if students don't engage in activities that reinforce their learning and performance levels from the previous year. Maintenance activities do not have to be classroom activities. There are a variety of workbook and technology opportunities, along with vendor programs for critical and creative thinking. These programs help maintain learning and performance levels over a long summer break and make it possible for teachers to begin introducing new skills and concepts earlier than they would normally.

- **Teambuilding Activities:** One of the foundations of a truly effective student-focused program is the development of teaching and learning teams. Summer offers an opportunity for teachers to meet new students and engage in activities that help forge teaching and learning teams. Sharing endurance of a challenge or sharing learning experience as peers can help students and teachers establish a rapport outside the constraints of classroom etiquette and expectations.

- **Standardizing Activities:** Students come to school with a wide variety of talents, strengths, and weaknesses. The development of a common repertoire of rituals, routines, and strategies can give all students an equal opportunity to become successful. Standardizing activities that build a common collection of strategies for success erase gaps that are a result of differences in life experience.

- **Talent or Interest Development:** Many students have abilities in music, art, or writing while others have talents in athletics or technologies. Programs that enable students to pursue talents with expert direction pay dividends and build student confidence, improve student attitude, and change student perceptions.

If teachers want to become serious about building a school that enables all students to be successful, they must examine the opportunities offered during the summer to do things that are not possible during the regular school year. Working with students to build a menu of summer activities in which students would participate pays dividends when teachers begin to reactivate students as learners during the Opening Period.

Summers are also crucial for teachers. They allow time for personal development and decompression. They allow teachers to build life experience with travel or professional activities outside the classroom teacher role. These are important and beneficial but they're not the only things that teachers can do in the summer.

TEACHERS IN THE SUMMER "OFF"

We often hear people talk about teachers having the summer off. If they are wise, they don't talk like this in front of teachers.

We often hear people talk about teachers having the summer off. If they are wise, they don't talk like this in front of teachers. Teachers have a number of growth opportunities for the summer — pursuing higher levels of education, travel, and cultural enrichment — but there are some school-related activities that cannot be performed at any other time of the year besides summer. These include:

1. **Student-Focused Professional Development:** Teachers need to be trained to continue to scaffold and push students as they become more proficient performers. To a great extent, this is student specific. Generic professional development is frequently program-related, strategy-related, or law-related. Teachers need to be candid about their ability to move the students they are going to have in class. If students are going to have attitude problems, teachers need to know how to help them. If students have low self-esteem and perception problems, teachers need to understand how that affects both learning and performing and know how to deal with it in the classroom. If students have attention deficit issues or if they can't actively listen or critically read, teachers need to be prepared to address it as a part of their unit and lesson planning. Schools and districts collect data points that can help identify students who are at-risk of not reaching proficiency.

2. **Outreach Activities:** Parents often tell researchers they feel that teachers don't care about them or their children. In our experience, this is not the case but is the perception of parents, especially parents of underperforming students. Reaching out precisely at the end of the summer to new students and their parents can provide opportunities for teachers to build rapport with both groups. This is important in communities where many parents have adversarial relationships with the school and teachers. It provides teachers with an opportunity to introduce effective parenting strategies in nonthreatening

and nonjudgmental ways. It also provides a vehicle for getting students engaged in the activities that were listed in the student section above.

3. **Curriculum and Data Management Plan:** We recommend a backward version of planning that begins with unpacking a standard to establish grade level exit expectations, and then developing lessons that will provide all students with the work that they need to move forward. This doesn't mean listing a standard or standards for each lesson. Rather, each lesson should move the students to the goals for the unit, and each unit should move students toward the goals for the year. This requires a different approach to data management and a different focus in PLC discussions.

4. **Access Building Activities:** These activities involve teachers working with the students they will have next year in a shared adventure or learning experience. They not only help broaden the experience base for both teacher and student, but they help create a rapport between teacher and student, and they can be a foundation for the development of teacher/learner teams that can come together as a workgroup to further learning. Access provides numerous benefits, not only academically but also in the area of behavior management. Many times, interacting with volatile students or students with behavior issues outside the classroom can defuse the students' default reaction to authority and create a relationship that will allow the student and teacher to dialogue and discuss problems instead of carrying on dual monologues that solve nothing. They also enable the teacher to use humor and reason to defuse situations instead of mandating adherence to rules and regulations.

5. **Educational Travel:** Many travel groups now offer trips specifically for teachers that emphasize building experience within

areas that the teacher will teach our areas that are particularly interesting to the teacher and contribute to personal development and growth. Educational travel can provide real-world examples to share with students that can broaden their perspective and increase their real-world connection.

6. **"Out of Comfort Zone" Experience:** These are experiences that take teachers out of their comfort zone, challenges them to do something that's very different to their normal school year routine, and can help teachers in several ways. It can provide them with a different perspective about what's going on in the world, it supports changes in brain activity, it increases critical and creative thinking activity, and it increases teacher confidence. This type of activity includes jobs outside education, jobs in education but in a very different role (grade level, leadership role, etc.), and experiences in a very different field (e.g., theater, athletics, or musical performances). Expanding the comfort zone of teachers tends to make them more flexible and more adaptable when they return to the classroom. Interestingly enough, "out of comfort zone" experiences have the same effect on students.

Many districts struggle to retain staff — especially quality staff — and are looking for ways to increase their retention rate. Helping teachers identify summer opportunities and secure funding and support can help change the teacher morale in a school and build a pipeline of master teachers and potential academic leaders for a school or district.

For administrators, the summer after the first Rhythm of the Learner Year will include most of the activities that they engaged in during the first summer — before they had a chance to experience trying to work with the Learner Year — but more in-depth involvement and more assessment of school and self. They will also find that a large number of new opportunities for self-assessment and planning are available.

After the first year, many academic leaders find that it is very easy to identify professional development needed to improve their craft. They also find that evaluating teachers moves to a whole different level, and they are more intentional and thoughtful when they observe and conference with teachers to develop personal growth plans.

Academic leaders can benefit from the same types of activities that are formative for teachers. However, in addition to formative and restorative activities, leaders have to understand that the activities planned for teachers and students during the summer must be implemented, monitored, and adjusted. (The latter applies if an activity isn't providing the desired results or is providing negative results.) For administrators, the second summer provides an opportunity for a choice between personal development and professional development while at the same time providing the academic leadership needed for the summer to be an effective teaching and learning experience for staff and students.

In this second summer, academic leaders and their teachers (to the extent possible) need to begin the summer with an assessment of the school's performance during the last year, the effectiveness of teacher and learner work in each of the periods of the Learner Year, and an assessment of what specific professional development activities will increase the performance in their role next year. This involves reviewing all of the evaluations done for each period during the year and identifying how each period was implemented and the impact of the implementation on learners.

This activity is the beginning of school planning for next year. The foundations for the school improvement plan, the professional development plan, and the academic support plan will all be developed during this discussion.

If time allows, leadership should be able to evaluate all academic and management systems and compare their current status to best practice. This will enable them to start planning how to change specific systems to make them more effective for supporting teaching and learning. Ed Directions' coaches encourage the analysis of several core systems during the second year, including:

- Planning.

- Program.

- Curriculum.

- Materials, texts, and technology selection.

- Instruction.

- Behavior management.

- Data management.

- Professional development.

- Bussing.

Evaluation of these core systems and identification of priority needs are steps in developing an intentional, *student* improvement plan and increases the intentionality and effectiveness of the *school* improvement plan.

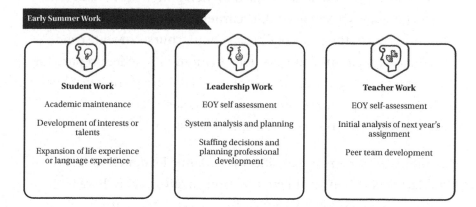

The experience of leading a school through the first year of adapting to the Rhythm of the Learner Year prepares academic leaders for a more focused late Summer Period. In addition to evaluating the teacher and student activities from the summer and doing an evaluation of the Summer Period, leaders have to begin finalizing their school improvement plan and developing action plans for at least the Opening Period and the Formative Period. These action plans will be translated into tactical plans that each staff member will develop to identify how the school improvement and action plans will affect their job responsibilities. These tactical plans can be used to drive observations and evaluate implementation.

Once school opens, administrators must juggle several different responsibilities. Final preparations of building, grounds, and classrooms for students must be completed. Systems have to be field-tested and working efficiently. Instructional materials — texts, technologies, and programs — need to be in place, and teachers need to be trained in their effective use and have time to link them to their unit and lesson plans.

Administrators have to keep the focus of teachers on one important understanding: moving the students from where they are to where they need to be is the goal of classroom work. This means that teachers develop unit lessons first and then pull the text, materials, and technologies that will enable learners to do the work that they must do to reach the goals of the class, unit, course, or state exam. This means that administrators need to monitor teacher preparation for classes to see if student development is the driver, or if teachers are relying on a pacing guide or curriculum lessons set that was developed by someone else for some other students.

Another important responsibility of academic leaders is to standardize the vision of an effective learning institution. If there are going to be schoolwide rituals and routines, these need to be explained, practiced by staff, and embedded in the first week's curriculum. During the first week, administrators need to monitor and provide feedback for teachers on the effectiveness of their academic and behavioral rituals and routines. This has to be planned and shared with the staff before the students arrive.

If teachers are going to have their own academic or behavioral rituals and routines, these need to be shared with academic leaders who can check to make sure that they are consistent with any schoolwide rituals and routines and with district and school policies and procedures. Before the first week of school, administrators also need to ensure that teachers' specific rituals and routines are consistent and compatible across content areas and grade levels.

If teachers do not understand the importance of rituals and routines in enabling student success or if they do not know how to implement, monitor, or judge their impact, they must have immediate ad hoc professional development provided by the academic leaders or by district specialists. (If Ed Directions is in the building, the Ed Directions coach could provide the professional development.)

Finally, academic leaders have to market the new vision of student-focused education to more than just staff. New staff, new parents, and new students need to have orientation that makes them aware of what the vision means and have ongoing support in reaching practitioner level — effective teacher strategies, effective parenting strategies, and effective student work. This means that academic leaders have to develop orientation and enculturating programs that begin before school starts, but are available to any new hires, new parents, or new students who come into the building.

As a rule, the further the school gets into the school year, the more at-risk new teachers, parents, and students will be if they start without any idea about what the school is trying to achieve.

In one school, the academic leaders decided that because only 30 percent of the students who started the year would finish the year in the school, they needed to have an ongoing orientation and enculturation program. Their plan included a room set aside for orienting new students. Students didn't go to regular classes for three days after they enrolled in the school. Instead, they were introduced to the school, to their classes, and to the work students were doing in class at the time. If they couldn't do the work, before or after school programs were available for the three days for the students to learn the skills they needed. The room was staffed by in-school suspension teachers who alternated morning and afternoon orientation programs. The program produced results as expected. Failures dropped and fewer students had to be enrolled in remedial support programs. Some results were unexpected — referrals for serious offenses dropped by almost 60 percent, and absentee rates dropped significantly. The school moved from at-risk status to successful status in one year.

Ed Directions' coaches emphasize that academic leaders need to make sure that the opening of school is successful. It has to be planned, marketed, and implemented so that all students finish the Opening Period knowing that they can be successful this year. Since the Formative Period follows directly on the heels of the Opening Period, all staff must understand the opportunity offered by the Formative Period for developing learners and improving student potential.

This also has to be planned and marketed before school starts so that teachers can be prepared, and they don't lose instructional momentum trying to make an unanticipated switch in focus. The preparation for a successful Formative Period begins with effective leadership in the weeks before school starts.

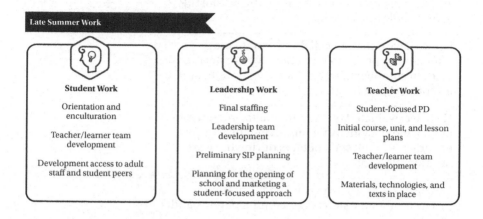

Evaluating the Summer Period

Best Practice Indicators	Yes/No	Priority
Did we evaluate our success in each of the periods of the Learner Year and use that evaluation to drive this year's SIP process?		
Did we create staff and student profiles and use those to help staff and students select formative summer programs?		
Did we provide the summer programs that we selected with the financial, human, and material resources needed to effectively implement, monitor, and evaluate the program?		
Did the leadership team secure the experience and professional development experiences needed for them to be more proficient in their roles?		
Did we formulate a vision of what the school was going to be like during the next school year, market that vision to all stakeholders, and provide support for stakeholders to develop the skills?		

Best Practice Indicators	Yes/No	Priority
Do we have the expertise on staff to implement all of the priority elements within the school SIP, action, and tactical plans?		
Do we have data that will demonstrate that our summer program had a positive impact on student competencies, teacher preparation, and intentional planning?		
Have we evaluated our summer data and developed a menu of ideas for improving the summer experience for all stakeholders during the next Summer Period?		
Did we provide orienting and enculturating programs for new staff and incoming parents and students?		
Do we have a plan in place for ongoing orientation and enculturating for new teachers and new students?		

Summer Period Planning

Period	Activity	Leader	Completion Date	Expected Outcome
Opening of Summer (June Plan)				

Additional Readiness Checklists for the Summer Period

Data Management

System Indicators	Yes/No	Priority
Our school data plan was designed with "best practice" in mind.		
The school has identified the performance expected of all students and identified the data streams needed to monitor and support those expectations.		
The school has acquired the technology and established the information management systems needed to capture the critical data elements.		
Teachers are surveyed regularly to determine if data systems are adequate to their needs.		
The school's data management system (DMS) is advanced enough to allow ad hoc queries and capture data stored in separate sub-systems.		
The DMS has been streamlined to facilitate daily entry and retrieval of data by teachers and administrators.		

Data Management

System Indicators	Yes/No	Priority
The DMS allows easy and timely transmission of data between/among role groups.		
Use of the DMS is regularly monitored and evaluated to determine frequency and impact of use.		
The school's DMS generates, collects, and organizes data needed to evaluate the success (or lack of) of school-wide (or district-wide) initiatives.		
The school's DMS allows the tracking/assisting of both individual students and targeted groups.		
The school's DMS enables teachers to relate/pattern the relationship between/among teacher work, student work, and student performance.		
Teachers have been trained and provided with the resources needed to use the DMS effectively.		
The data collected/generated is analyzed and shared by multiple role groups.		
The school uses data to identify and/or evaluate intervention strategies, materials, and plan priorities.		
All plans incorporate and are based on current student performance data.		

Performance Assessment

System Indicators	Yes/No	Priority
Our school performance assessment plan was designed with our school's "best practice" in mind.		
The school culture recognizes ongoing assessment of student performance as an important data generation tool and a significant learning activity.		
School policies establish and support "best practice" assessment strategies for both the school and individual classrooms.		
All teachers have been trained in "best practices" for the development, administration, scoring and analysis, and follow up of tests.		
The school test plan includes "real-time" scrimmages to generate performance data and prepare students for state and national tests.		
School assessment includes timely scrimmages (formative and summative) to track student mastery and target students for assistance.		
Technologies are used to facilitate data management and save time in generating, organizing, analyzing, and communicating data.		
Assessment is designed to establish the level at which students have mastered the knowledge, task/process, and application expectations.		
The difficulty and complexity of school and class assessments escalate to the levels of state and national assessments before those tests are given.		
Teacher-made tests prepare all students for the format, venue, language, duration, and language issues found in state tests.		
Teacher-made tests include diagnostic elements to identify the level of success and/or causes of failure to reach expectations.		

Performance Assessment

System Indicators	Yes/No	Priority
School assessments include a variety formats beyond "pencil and paper" to encourage success in nontraditional performers.		
All student work (not just tests) is scored and, if not at student potential or if not proficient, is analyzed to establish the breakdown and the cause.		
All assessment results are collected and analyzed, and patterns of performance are communicated to all staff.		
Support systems are revised as new data are analyzed and indicate a need for change in priorities.		
School and teacher assessment practices are monitored to make sure school policies are followed.		
The school assessment plan is reviewed regularly and is revised when change is needed to approach "best practice."		

Student Management

System Indicators	Yes/No	Priority
Our school student management system was designed with our school's "best practice" in mind.		
The community sees the school as a safe and secure environment with a strong learner focus.		
The community is involved in and strongly supports school efforts in behavior management.		
The school culture emphasizes the importance of all students being highly engaged in effective work.		
The school research has identified, defined, and planned for student behaviors associated with optimal student performance.		
The school has a policy in place to support "best practice" discipline, attendance, and support programs.		
A data management plan was designed to enable the regular review of policy and procedures to determine buy-in, effectiveness, and equity.		
A "code of conduct" has been published and communicated to all stakeholders. Student rights, responsibilities, and expectations are included.		
Teachers have been trained to use proactive management and to avoid escalating encounters with students.		
The school provides time and assistance for teachers to develop, monitor, and refine rituals, routines, and management procedures.		
All teachers have translated the code of conduct into their class rituals, routines, and expectations. Expectations are posted and used proactively.		

Student Management

System Indicators	Yes/No	Priority
The school collects and analyzes data to identify patterns (time, location, student mix) that lead to non-productive behaviors.		
Interventions (pattern and individual) are proactive and formative with an emphasis on maintaining the teaching/learning process.		
Individual punishment is appropriate, consistent, and is evaluated for effectiveness.		
The school's student management plan is regularly reviewed and is adjusted as needed to maintain optimal behaviors.		
School use of technologies enables quick communication, collection, and organization of data, and enables effective monitoring of critical areas.		
The school works with PTA/PTO groups to inform parents about effective parenting strategies for different age groups.		

Time Management

System Indicators	Yes/No	Priority
Our school's time management culture was designed with "best practice" in mind.		
Existing rituals, routines, programs, and events not working efficiently are identified. Those not supporting improved performance are abandoned.		
The school's planning process accurately estimated the time needed for role groups to plan, implement, and evaluate the critical elements of the plan.		
There is a "master calendar" that sets expectations for beginning, ending, and evaluating impact of major initiatives.		
The school is able to provide the time needed to address unforeseen issues in a timely manner.		
Blocks of common time are available for groups or teams who work together. Needed student data and profiles are available.		
All role groups have been trained in and use "effective meeting procedures."		
Technologies have been integrated into all classrooms to support teaching, learning, and the management of student performance data.		
All role groups have been trained in use of technology to reduce time spent on tasks not related to improved student performance.		
Bell schedules, transit patterns, management programs, and class schedules have been designed to maximize teaching and learning time.		
Time "sponges" (e.g., paperwork, reports, or activities) not related to teaching/learning process have been eliminated, reallocated, or rescheduled.		

Time Management

System Indicators	Yes/No	Priority
Classroom time is not lost to ineffective class-room rituals, discipline problems, or ineffective student work patterns.		
Institutional interruptions (e.g., intercom, announcements, etc.) are purposeful, timely, and kept to a minimum.		
Students are aware of the importance of "time on task" and are involved in efforts to increase efficiency.		
Time utilization is regularly audited to identify more efficient ways to spend time for teaching and learning.		

10

CONCLUSION

In the introduction, the we emphasized that this book would focus on building a schedule around the students, taking them from where they were to where they needed to be before the annual assessment. We noted that adopting this particular approach to education required that academic leaders question conventional wisdom and rethink their priorities for strategic planning.

We highlighted that certain understandings were fundamental to this approach — the nature of standards, how students learn, and what causes them to perform at the level they do. This set of understandings is fundamental to the development of the concept of embracing the Rhythm of the Learner Year.

We introduced the Learner Year and, in the following chapters, examined in detail each period. As part of this development, we tried to redefine what was "best practice" for leadership, for teachers, and most importantly, for students. In each chapter, we examined academic leadership (not just management), student-focused teacher work, and the importance of effective student learning work. Each period had its priorities.

SUMMER

In the first summer, leadership priorities are somewhat limited because of the lack of necessary causal data for students and teachers from the preceding year. Priorities around evaluation of school systems and the development of a vision of a school based on a Learner Year are the two most critical competencies. Without this activity set, school leaders will follow the traditional practice, which emphasizes reforming based on adult behaviors rather than student need.

Academic leadership in the first summer focuses on getting the building and staff ready, building a vision of a new culture, and a plan for rolling out that new culture as the teachers and students come back to school.

OPENING SCHOOL

Building the groundwork for effective learning and performing is critical if we want students to acquire large amounts of content and to learn to use that content in rigorous, complex tasks. This building begins in the Opening Period, and if it's ignored, teachers can find themselves living in a world that doesn't support behaving, learning, or performing. We emphasized that we don't win the year in the opening, but if we ignore the students' needs, we can lose the year in the first three weeks of school.

For teachers to be successful, they must take care of the compliance business — forms need to be filled out, and rosters need to be completed. Sometimes in this rush to compliance, teachers miss out on their opportunity to design the culture and climate of their classroom. Students need a safe and welcoming environment if we are going to get all students on board and moving toward proficiency. Students will design their own culture and climate around their expectations for behavior and work unless rapport is established, etiquette for adult-to-student interaction is built, and academic and behavior rituals, routines, and expectations are established to support the development of learning and performing by the third week of school.

FORMATION OF LEARNERS

In an effective Formative Period, students can grow their potential significantly and acquire and create meaning for a large body of content. They can also become more proficient at using content to perform tasks and can grow with those tasks as the tasks increase in rigor and complexity.

The third period of the Learner Year focuses on the formation of the proficient learner. If teachers want students to acquire and own content — concepts and skills — they have to build a sequence of student work that enables the students to attend (learning begins with attention) and acquire (the student has to do work to acquire since the teacher cannot acquire for the student).

The learning must be organized, or it doesn't reach long-term memory. If it's organized, the student has to do work (usually thinking about content) that creates meaning for what's been learned. Meaningful work is the key to independent retrieval of what's been learned in response to language cues.

This is impossible if the school hasn't opened effectively, if rituals and routines are not in place to establish optimal behaviors and patterns of student work, and if teachers aren't monitoring student growth and providing immediate targeted assistance for at-risk students. An ineffective opening can make it impossible for teachers to teach and students to learn at the levels required for students to make adequate growth during this period.

CALIBRATION OF PERFORMANCE

The Calibrating Period offers the opportunity for teachers to build proficient performers (i.e., students who can use what they've learned at the levels required by a state assessment or by an end-of-year exam). During the Calibrating Period, student work escalates gradually, moving students to the levels of endurance, rigor, complexity, and thinking that are consistent with "proficient" standards-based performance.

Calibration is all about preparing students to reach their potential as performers. With effective Opening and Formative Periods, it is possible to get almost all students to their potential by the time of the test. The more ineffective the previous periods, the fewer students will reach their potential. In extreme cases, it may not be possible to build a systemic program of performance development, in which case teachers will have to use a variety of "triage strategies" to solve priority needs that can be solved quickly.

GETTING BEST EFFORT ON THE TEST

The Testing Period is, as one of the Ed Directions coaches put it, "the proof in the pudding." In a best-practice world, all students will have learned, and they will be able to demonstrate how well they've learned to the level of proficiency on the state test or EOY assessment. The Testing Period is related to school accountability. A state test is how people "keep score" on schools. Academic leaders must understand the importance of an effective Testing Period.

Conventional wisdom emphasizes that administrators do the required "compliance procedures" (i.e., ethical considerations and testing rules and procedures). They develop a schedule, distribute students, follow the schedule, administer the test, pick up the test, and send it back. This is different than the Testing Period described in this book. We talk about not only doing things right but doing the right things to establish an optimal environment for students.

In the Rhythm of the Learner Year, the development of testing plans goes beyond compliance and focuses on building an optimal environment to make it possible for a school to get a "grade" that represents the real potential of their learners and performers. What our coaches have found is that schools that merely comply most often get student performance that is inconsistent with the student potential. The school score is a "false read" that may be far removed from actual student potential. We emphasize that you can't win the game during the Testing Period, but you can lose it if you don't plan for success.

An effective testing plan may involve operation outside the normal operating procedure. Schedules may have to be changed, students may have to be redistributed, and rooms may have to be reorganized if we want all students to operate at "best effort."

Culture and climate are particularly important. A toxic climate or a classroom where the student-teacher relationship is adversarial can be disastrous in terms of student performance.

STARTING NEXT YEAR THIS YEAR

The EOY Period is important for planning for next year. Leadership and instructional staff can evaluate the periods of this Learner Year, identify strengths and concerns, analyze academic and non-academic systems to identify which need to be redesigned or tweaked for better efficiency, and plan for needed professional development. This is the beginning of next year's strategic action plan and the beginning of each staff person's development of their tactical action plan for next year.

We emphasize that the EOY needs to be planned so that students own their learnings and are recognized for their achievements. This is an important developmental process for students. It helps build attitude, perception, and thinking that support learning and performing in the next grade.

While we don't lose the game in the EOY Period, we can miss an opportunity to build quality plans for the adults in the building and provide activities that will be beneficial to the students during the summer.

KEEPING MOMENTUM ALL SUMMER LONG

After the first summer working with the Rhythm of the Learner Year, summer activities for academic leaders, instructional staff, and students can be much more intentional and focused on building proficient learners and performers. It's possible to do a more informed evaluation of all school systems (starting with culture and climate) and to do a more effective job of planning professional development.

Building informed, strategic plans that focus on student development, marketing those plans to all stakeholders, and preparing the building, the staff, and the students to implement the plans becomes the story arc for an effective summer program.

After the first summer, if school leadership attends to maintaining the momentum of the Learner Year — of the leadership work, of the teacher work, and of the student work — the school can make tremendous gains each year for several years.

In one case, a district that never had a successful school — all schools had earned "F's" every year — had a new superintendent who adopted the Rhythm of the Learner Year as the district focus. In the first year, six of 10 were successful and three more were nearly successful. In the second year, nine of the 10 were rated as highly successful. In a low performing school (always an F or sometimes a D), a principal saw the potential of the Rhythm of the Learner Year, marketed it to staff, and then marketed it to elementary students. At the end of the first year, the school was a B. In the second year, it was an A and remained an A as long as that principal stayed in the school.

FINAL THOUGHTS

For readers of this book, it's important to remember that the Rhythm of the Learner Year is not a recipe book that is to be followed step-by-step or a new product to be marketed. Rather, it is an introduction to a student-focused approach to the educator's craft. We understand that integration and implementation of the suggestions developed in the chapters will look different from school to school and even from class to class.

It's important to remember that the Rhythm of the Learner Year is not a recipe book that is to be followed step-by-step or a new product to be marketed. Rather, it is an introduction to a student-focused approach to the educator's craft.

The whole story arc of the book revolves around the idea that if all students are to be successful, adults must honor their work, their needs, and their schedules.

If all students are to be successful, adults must honor their work, their needs, and their schedules.

Following this theme, it is important to emphasize that the appendices included in the book are not designed to be a "one-size-fits-all" toolkit. Think of it as a carpenter's toolbox. The carpenter does not use all the tools in the box on every job. As a professional, the carpenter uses the ones he (or she) needs. We intended that readers would check out the tools connected to the chapters, select tools that they can use, and leave the others until they become useful.

APPENDIX 1: ADDITIONAL SUMMER TOOLS

FACILITIES CHECKLIST

1. **Walking tour of grounds**
   - Construction and repair sites are secured.
   - Signs, billboards, etc. in good repair and up to date.
   - Grounds, play areas, parking areas are attractive and in good repair.
   - The outside of the building and windows are attractive and in good repair.
   - Grounds needs-assessment and wish list completed and requested or scheduled.

2. **Building interior**
   - Scheduled repair or construction is underway and will be completed on time.
   - All exterior doors and locks are in good working order and secured.
   - All interior doors are in good repair and can be secured.
   - Main office area is clean, convenient, and user-friendly.
   - Main office technologies have been checked, are in good working order, and are adequate to meet the needs of office staff.

- Cafeteria is clean, inspected, and organized for convenient entry and exit.
- Library is secure, up-to-date, and materials and technologies are available for teacher and student use.
- The auditorium/gym/all-purpose room has been checked and is clean and in good repair. All equipment is in good repair and is sufficient to meet the needs of academic and special area teachers and students.
- Gym and recreational equipment have been audited and provide opportunities for all students to be engaged in appropriate physical activities.
- Automobile/bus/walker entry and exit points have been checked for safety and efficiency of movement.

3. **Classrooms**
   - All classrooms have been inspected, and safety or health concerns have been identified and scheduled for repair.
   - All classrooms are equipped with adequate technologies for teachers to move students to the levels defined by state standards.
   - Teachers in grade-level teams have examined their classrooms and requested and received adequate furniture and equipment to enable flexible organization as needed to facilitate teacher and student work.
   - All classrooms are clean and have safety information posted in a prominent position.

FACILITIES NEEDS LIST

Facility Checklist

Area/Issue/Date	Action(s) Needed	Request Sent To/Date	Completion/Date Schedule/Actual
Grounds			
Interior			
Classrooms			

TEACHER TRANSLATION ACTIVITY WORKSHEET

What parts of this plan require change(s) in my job/classroom?

_____

_____

What parts of the plan will be my top priority?

_____

_____

What specific plan activities will I implement and when will they be completed?

_____

_____

Activity	Start	Completion	Evaluation

What will be the impact on my students' work/performance?

_____

_____

To be successful, I will need ...

_____

_____

I would like you to check my progress ... (when?) (how often?)

_____

_____

APPENDIX 2: ADDITIONAL OPENING OF SCHOOL TOOLS

CLASS MAKEUP – ISSUES AND BARRIERS TO SUCCESS OF "AT-RISK" STUDENTS

Lack of Academic Success

Critical Group	Number	Students
One year behind core group		
Two or more years behind core group		

Discipline

Critical Group	Number	Students
Multiple serious offenses		
Multiple class-room disruptions		
Multiple tardiness		

Attendance

Critical Group	Number	Students
1 to 5 days		
6 to 10 days		
11 to 20 days		
21 days or more		

Performance

Critical Group	Number	Students
Scored a "1" in a content area		
Scored a "1" in more than one content area		
Has never scored above a "1"		

Opening Period Observation: Teacher

Date: _____ Teacher: _____ Period: _____ Observer: _____

	Teacher Work	Student Work
5 Mins		
10 Mins		
15 Mins		
20 Mins		

Teacher Work Analysis

Design	Execution	Quality
• Academic ritual/ routine • Behavior ritual/ routine • Focused on student performance expected • Differentiated materials and technologies • Differentiated delivery • Differentiated student work • Checks for learning	• Lesson plan, critical learnings, and materials ready • Teacher started class promptly and made smooth transitions • Academic rituals modeled or practiced • Teacher kept all students highly engaged in work • Teacher kept most students highly engaged in work • Student engagement monitored and corrective feedback given by teacher	• High quality — all student and teacher work effective • Mix high quality and adequate teacher and student work • Adequate student and teacher work • Mix adequate teacher work and inadequate student work • Inadequate teacher work/plan • Both inadequate

Notes: _____

_____

Opening Period Observation: Students

Date: _____ Teacher: _____ Period: _____ Observer: _____

	Teacher Work	Student Work
5 Mins		
10 Mins		
15 Mins		
20 Mins		

Student Engagement Analysis

Work Task	Venue	Student Engagement
• Attending • Acquiring • Translation/ organization • Creating meaning • Calibrating • Assessment • Challenge activity • Guided practice • Revision to proficiency	• Whole class lecture • Textbook work, worksheet, or handout • Facilitated practice • Learner groups • Performer groups • Performance/ritual practice • Differentiated strategies	• All students highly engaged • Most highly engaged • Some highly engaged, rest engaged • All engaged or compliant • Most engaged, the rest off-task • All off task

Notes: _____

_____

APPENDIX 3: ADDITIONAL FORMATIVE TOOLS AND STUDENT WORK SAMPLES

ORGANIZING WORK – CRITICAL LEARNINGS OF A SHAPE

Many students are not prepared with the thinking or learning competencies needed to be successful learners and performers. If the class starts covering the content from day one and proceeds on a set schedule determined by a committee, students who lack competencies will quickly realize they cannot be successful. Many will give up. To offset this, we recommend teachers use directed activities in the Formative Period. Directed work (learning work, thinking work, reading work, writing work, or assessment work) can build student competence and confidence by providing a "guided walk-through" that ensures that the student does the work correctly before they're asked to do it independently.

Using directed activities, teachers address their content and, at the same time, build student competence and confidence; they embed activities in the student work that increase the students' mastery of learning and performing. In the Formative Period, we encourage teachers to use DLAs (directed learning activities), DTAs (directed thinking activities), DRAs (directed reading activities), and DWAs (directed writing activities) to equip students with strategies and structures enabling them to learn and use the content critical in the unit or lesson. We use the information sheet included below to help teachers build directed activities in the Opening Period or early in the Formative Period, so the students develop the competencies needed for independent application in the Calibrating Period.

Directed Strategy	Definition	Impact on Student Potential
Directed Learning Activities	Attending to learning Acquiring learning Organizing learning Creating meaning for learning	Building specific learning work strategies for all students prepares them to engage the learning process with minimum competencies in place. It may take time for some students to master all of the strategies but using the strategies will ensure progressively more of the learnings make it into long-term memory.
Directed Thinking Activities	Critical thinking Creative thinking Problem solving Decision-making	Providing students with directed thinking work helps build mature thinking patterns in students whose thinking has not matured enough for them to perform at the level of expectations. Directed thinking activities engage students in thinking about or thinking with content and create meaning for the content.

Directed Strategy	Definition	Impact on Student Potential
Directed Reading Activities	Reading to learn Reading to critique Reading to analyze	Thoughtful or purposeful reading is required on every question on every state test. Students who become efficient recreational readers but never develop strategies for close or critical reading can read for the "mental movie" but not read analytically and respond thoughtfully to what they have read. Students must have a menu of reading strategies to equip them for the types of reading expected in state standards.
Directed Writing Activities	Writing to learn Writing to persuade Writing to inform Writing to give directions Writing to teach	Critical writing is assessed in any testing situation where open-response or extended-response questions are included and are heavily weighted. The ability to use words to express thinking and convey ideas or emotions is not only tested but is a large part of the exit expectations for each grade level. A menu of writing strategies not only makes the student a more effective communicator, but it also plays an important part of developing the student as a learner.

Directed activities are important in the early stages of the Formative Period. Building collective competencies helps erase gaps in prior experience between and among students. It provides a competency core, enabling all students who give best effort to be successful. It is important to note, while the directed activities build the foundation for student as learner, in the Formative Period it will be equally important for us to make the student an independent learner and use the foundation work created by the directed strategies to build the student aptitude. In the Formative Period, we look for a developmental process that might follow this pattern:

Step 1: Introduction to a strategy with teacher modeling and collective use.

Step 2: Student use with direction or alerts provided by the teacher.

Step 3: Independent use with teacher monitoring and giving shaping feedback.

Step 4: Independent identification of critical learnings and development of personalized strategies.

Step 5: Independent identification of critical learnings, development of personal strategies, and self-assessment and revision of strategies as needed.

In an ideal situation, all students would become masters of directed activities and self-directed learners by the end of the Formative Period. Some will not make that jump. However, the process will enable almost all students to acquire and use learnings in more rigorous and complex activities.

Students who are not independent by the end of the Formative Period will need to start the Calibrating Period with a very targeted support system for building independence.

————————————

Planning the student work in a Formative Period then becomes a critical task for teachers. Because of the amount of content, the number of tasks, and the complexity of the competencies required on state assessments, lessons must be efficient, focused, and effective. "Time off-task" not only breaks instructional and learning momentum but also costs the class time that could be used in expanding their work experience.

In the Formative Period, there are specific strategies that are considered best practice. These activities maximize classroom time for students to be engaged in effective work and offer the opportunity to build competencies and attitudes consistent with proficient work in the Calibrating Period.

Teachers also need to understand that they can design effective work, but the way that work plays out in class may determine whether it is indeed effective. Just assigning effective work does not guarantee all students will benefit from the work. In the Formative Period, especially the first half of the Formative Period, mastery of behavior management rituals and routines is as important as the mastery of academic rituals and routines. Classes that are disrupted or lose focus because of behavior can have well-planned work for students but miss creating maximum impact because of the breaks in the flow of teaching and learning.

We have identified specific work patterns that encourage effective interaction by all students in formative work:

Formative Period: Supporting Student Learning Work

Work Pattern	Definition	Impact on Students
Identification of the purpose and expected outcomes of the student work.	Work that establishes purpose. Work that establishes what's to be learned and what the students are accountable for when they demonstrate learning.	Establishes a defined set of parameters for the learnings that build student competency and confidence and links learning to performance. Intentional work builds independence and confidence.
Establishment of the activity etiquette and the behavior and engagement expectations for the class.	Work that allows students to identify the behavior and engagement expectations for the activity or task.	Defines the expectations for optimal classwork. It establishes student accountability for behavior and engagement and encourages high-level engagement for the duration of an activity.
Identification of an appropriate strategy and using the strategy to perform the task.	Work that prepares a student to use a thinking, writing, or other complex process to perform tasks on assessments or projects. This may be a directed activity if the students lack proficiency.	Provides foundation work for strategic thinking and for developing critical reading, writing, and thinking. Strategies support immature thinkers and provide a framework for future development.
Work preparation that causes a student to analyze a task and identify all of the steps to complete the assignment.	Work that prepares a student to do a task analysis. This is a preliminary step to mastering thoughtful responses that matches the purpose and required actions of a task.	Ensures student development of a strategy for thoughtful response to instructions or directions and plan work to completion.

Work Pattern	Definition	Impact on Students
Opportunities demonstrate high-level engagement and best-effort formative work.	Work that focuses on building the students' ability to engage in work and give best practice effort.	Encourages the student commitment to best effort and high-level engagement. Like athletes, students must build attitude, perception, and endurance. High-level engagement will be required for students to accomplish what they need to do in the Calibrating Period.
Work in the formal, discipline-specific language for concepts and tasks.	Work that forms the students' vocabulary and shapes the students' work in formal and discipline specific activities.	Moves students from informal language to formal register expectations. Tests are written in the language of the discipline, so all students need familiarity with formal, discipline-specific language.
Content literacy work that helps the students build mental models and constructs that create meaning.	Work that helps organize or link language to mental models and helps the students independently locate and use learning from long-term memory.	Builds students' confidence and competence in using long-term memory and prepare students to accept the challenge of a cumulative EOY assessment.

Work Pattern	Definition	Impact on Students
A classroom culture that emphasizes endurance, work to completion, and self-checking.	Work gradually expands endurance, willingness to work to completion, and self-checking ensures that all students engage in and seek proficiency in their formative work.	By the end of the Formative Period, students must be able to stay highly engaged for up to 15 minutes, complete all tasks, and revise work to proficiency. Most need formative work to reach this level for the Calibrating Period.
Using shaping feedback with revision to proficiency to improve work.	Work that establishes what needs to be done to student product to make it proficient and then supports student revision to proficiency.	Helps students understand that a product isn't finished until it's proficient. Accepting feedback and working to revise are habits of mind required of proficient students.
Daily experience with proficient learning — attend, acquire, organize, and create meaning.	Work that engages the students in the critical Formative Period forms and provides an opportunity for feedback and revision.	Helps students overcome the idea that learning is the teacher's job and develops proficiency in the effective formative work patterns. This encourages confidence and competence and has a positive impact on attitude and perception.

Work Pattern	Definition	Impact on Students
Regular engagement in thinking work, problem-solving, and decision-making.	Critical work for establishing meaning but also for creating thoughtful responders as opposed to impulsive thinkers and responders.	Deep thinking helps build thoughtfulness and establishes multiple access lanes to memory. It is critical for the development of the thinking competencies, confidence competence, and independent thinking.
Critical reading, writing, and thinking work daily.	Work that engages the students in work that is critical to the development of mature thinking patterns.	Successful students can critically read, critically write, and critically think. They have strategies for purposeful and thoughtful development of ideas.

Another element of the early Formative Period is the linking of student learning work to student performance on an assessment. The Ed Directions coaches use the student assessment analysis set included below to identify areas of underperformance on a test and then use the follow-up PLC guide to check student preparation against student performance.

Once the teachers have identified the questions that a significant number of students missed, they can select student test samples and analyze the student learning work that should have prepared the students for the question. This allows them to determine if the students actually did the work, if they completed the work, and if their completed work was proficient and adequate preparation for the assessment. This allows the PLC team or the academic leadership team to assess the design, implementation, and impact of lessons on student performance and support teachers and students who are struggling.

Unit: _____   Date of Test: _____   Percent who Passed: _____

Question	Type	Task	Content	Students Who Missed
1	• Multiple choice • Fill in the blanks • Short answer • Extended answer • Response to text or data • Real world application • Problem solving/decision making • Writing prompt • Critical thinking or critical reading prompt	• Recall • Operation or procedure • Real world application • Response to data • Response to visual analysis or critique • Draw an inference or conclusion		
2	• Multiple choice • Fill in the blanks • Short answer • Extended answer • Response to text or data • Real world application • Problem solving/decision making • Writing prompt • Critical thinking or critical reading prompt	• Recall • Operation or procedure • Real world application • Response to data • Response to visual analysis or critique • Draw an inference or conclusion		

Question	Type	Task	Content	Students Who Missed
3	• Multiple choice • Fill in the blanks • Short answer • Extended answer • Response to text or data • Real world application • Problem solving/decision making • Writing prompt • Critical thinking or critical reading prompt	• Recall • Operation or procedure • Real world application • Response to data • Response to visual \ analysis or critique • Draw an inference or conclusion		
4	• Multiple choice • Fill in the blanks • Short answer • Extended answer • Response to text or data • Real world application • Problem solving/decision making • Writing prompt • Critical thinking or critical reading prompt	• Recall • Operation or procedure • Real world application • Response to data • Response to visual analysis or critique • Draw an inference or conclusion		

Linking Work

Prompt: We have been discussing "umbrella terms." One of the terms we used was "elements of a story."

What are the critical learnings that fall under the umbrella of "elements of a story?"

Concepts or Ideas	Tasks

Choose three of the learnings from your list and create one multiple choice question, one short answer question, and one open response question.

Multiple Choice	Short Answer	Open Response

Linking Work

Prompt: Read the accompanying selection, follow the instructions, and answer the questions below.

In the selection, the author explains why she thinks George Washington supported the Constitution of the United States. Use the four-column method to plan your answer so that you get full credit (one half your score) and then write your answer (one half your score).

The author identifies what she thinks is the cause of Washington's decision.

_____

_____

What is a cause?

_____

_____

What does the author identify as the cause of Washington's decision? What reasons does she use to show that this was indeed a cause?

_____

_____

Provide a quote from the selection that supports your reasoning.

_____

_____

Plan your four-column analysis below:

What is the question about?	**What do I have to do?**	**What will my answer include?**	**How can I improve my answer?**

Write your answer here:

_____

_____

Linking Work

On yesterday's test, we had to read a diagram and some text about a science experiment. We talked about how this is a more difficult question than multiple choice or short answer because it requires more thinking and a deeper understanding of science.

Today, I am going to give each of your work groups one of the units we studied in the first semester, and you will have to create a question that involves a diagram and some text about the subject of that unit. Use the flow chart below as a guide to developing your question.

Review the Unit	Select Learnings	Select a Diagram and Text	Design and Write Your Question	Give Your Question to Another Group to Answer and Critique	Finalize Your Question

Write your question below:

_____

_____

Meaningful Work – Critical Learnings of a Shape

Shape	Drawing	Features	Formulas We Learned
Rectangle		Four sides Right angles Diagonals equal	P = Side-Side-Side-Side

APPENDIX 4: ADDITIONAL CALIBRATING TOOLS AND STUDENT WORK SAMPLES

EXAMPLES OF CALIBRATING WORK

Student work in the Calibrating Period is designed to enable every student to perform to their potential on a cumulative, complex, rigorous assessment. This means that the work has to enable the students to work independently out of long-term memory, give best effort on questions (even if they are both challenging and outside the students' comfort zone), endure the assessment, and complete all tasks and self-assess to see if they can improve the level of work or the precision of the answer.

CRITICAL READING

Prompt: Read the selection provided to determine the main idea and find at least three important details that support the main idea. Once you have finished, read the following questions and write your answers in the space provided.

What was the main idea?

_____

_____

How did you decide this was the main idea? What were the clues that led to your decision?

_____

_____

Identify three important details that led you to believe this is the main idea:

1. _____

2. _____

3. _____

ORGANIZING FOR A PURPOSE

The first 10 amendments to the United States Constitution are called the Bill of Rights. As we study the amendments, use the chart below to organize our learnings. After we have studied all 10, each work group will be asked to determine which two are most important to today's issues. You will be able to discuss the prompt with your collaborative group but individually be asked to write your own SRE (Statement Reasons Evidence) response.

Amendment	Rights Guaranteed	Importance

Directed Learning – The Calibrating Period

Directed Strategy	Definition	Impact on Student Potential
Directed Learning Activities	Student work experiences that build proficiency in: • Attending to learning • Acquiring learning • Organizing learning • Creating meaning for learning • Linking learning to assessments • Linking current and prior learnings • Linking current learnings with standards expectations	Building specific learning work strategies prepares all students to engage in the learning process with minimum competencies in place. It may take time for some students to master all the strategies, but using the strategies will ensure that progressively more of the learnings make it into long-term memory. The addition of the linking activities to the learning strand enables students to understand both the expectations of the standards and the accountability of students under the standards.
Directed Thinking Activities (DTAs)	Student work experiences that provide strategies for an experience in: • Critical thinking • Creative thinking • Problem solving • Decision making • Strategic planning • Convergent and divergent thinking	Providing students with DTAs helps build mature thinking patterns in students whose thinking has not matured enough for them to perform at the level of expectations. DTAs engage students in thinking about or thinking with content and create meaning for the content. The addition of strategic planning, as well as convergent and divergent thinking activities, prepares students to pull together information from different resources or identify alternative possibilities and approach difficult situations or questions with confidence and competence.

Directed Strategy	Definition	Impact on Student Potential
Directed Reading Activities (DRAs)	Student work experiences that form proficient readers. Strategies for close reading and critical reading build a number of competencies in students': • Reading to learn • Reading to critique • Reading to analyze • Using structural and language analysis to unlock meaning • Seeking clarity and precision • Integrating information from multiple representations or resources • Reading and prioritizing data in response to a prompt	Thoughtful or purposeful reading is required on every question on every state test. Students who become efficient recreational readers but never develop strategies for close or critical reading can read for the "mental movie" but not read analytically or respond thoughtfully to what they have read. Students must have a menu of reading strategies to equip them for the types of reading expected in state standards. In addition, literacy requires students to develop habits of mind and specific strategies for getting beyond the literal meaning. The reading strand includes reading more than just text, and many of the questions involve text plus other representations of ideas.

Directed Strategy	Definition	Impact on Student Potential
Directed Writing Activities (DWAs)	For most students, writing is a stream of consciousness activity. Many see writing as creative writing; instead, they must develop strategies for the types of writing expected on assessments. Writing to: • Learn • Persuade • Inform • Give directions • Teach • Communicate thinking • Support a decision • Critique a selection or solution • Demonstrate learning • Demonstrate understanding • Clarify or communicate with precision	Critical writing is assessed in any testing situation where open response or extended response questions are included and are heavily weighted. The ability to use words to express thinking and convey ideas or emotions is not only tested but is a large part of the exit expectations for each grade level. A menu of writing strategies not only makes the student a more effective communicator but also plays an important part in developing the student as a learner. Again, state requirements for literacy emphasize more than just free composition or formulaic writing. The focus is on purposeful writing in which the writer uses language to communicate with self or with a reader for a particular purpose. DWAs build the menu of strategies as habits of mind needed by writers to communicate effectively.

The use of Directed Activities in the Calibrating Period moves beyond building basic learning competencies and focuses on building a menu of strategic patterns and habits of mind that support effective thinking and communication. Directed Activities enable us to build the set of competencies students need to take learnings into high-level assessments and real-world scenarios with confidence and effectiveness. The combination of basic learning strategies, thinking and test-taking strategies, and strategic management of information to develop a response is what is expected in state standards and demanded by real-world employers. We recommend a gradual release approach to Directed Activities in the Calibrating Period.

Step 1: Introduction to a strategy or approach with teacher modeling and collective use.

Step 2: Student use with direction or alerts provided by the teacher.

Step 3: Student use in peer performance situations.

Step 4: Independent use with teacher monitoring and rubric-based shaping feedback.

Step 5: Independent use with rubric-based self-assessment and revision to proficiency.

Step 6: Independent identification of critical learnings and development of personalized strategies.

Step 7: Independent identification of critical learnings, development of personal strategies, and self-assessment and revision of strategies as needed.

Using Directed Activities, teachers can continue to develop students as learners and build student work that shapes attitude, perception, and thinking. In the Calibrating Period, we continue to encourage teachers to use DLAs, DTAs, DRAs, and DWAs to equip students with strategies and structures that enable them to learn and perform. At this point, we also add DAAs (Directed Assessment Activities), rubric use and self-assessment strategies, test taking acumen, strategic thinking activities, and cumulative or capstone activities.

The goal of Directed Activities in the Calibrating Period is not the teaching of a strategy or approach. The goal is a continuation of the development of the independent learner and performer that was started in the Formative Period. By the end of the Calibrating Period, we want students to independently identify the learnings that are being assessed, identify what they must do to be proficient, perform the required tasks, and then self-check to see if their work reaches the level of proficiency required.

CALIBRATING STUDENT WORK SAMPLES

Critical Reading

Prompt: Read the selection provided to determine the main idea and find at least three important details that support the main idea. Once you have finished, read the following questions and write your answers in the space provided.

What was the main idea?

_____

_____

How did you decide this was the main idea? What were the clues that led to your decision?

_____

_____

Identify three important details that led you to believe this is the main idea:

1. _____

2. _____

3. _____

ACKNOWLEDGMENTS

Frank and Joe would like to express our heartfelt gratitude to all those who helped make this book possible. Our colleagues, partners, mentors, mentees, and the schools and districts with which we worked, all played a part in the evolution of our student-focused approach to a just-in-time Learner Year and the content of this book. Their feedback and suggestions about tools and additional insights they sought were critical to making this second volume in the Turning Around Turnaround Schools series user-friendly for educational practitioners.

In particular, we would like to thank our editors, Jessica Gardner and Kate Colbert, for making our manuscript even stronger, as well as our internal editing team: Susan Draus, Heather Tolle, Iam Bennett, Dr. Robert Johnson, and Jo Zouch. We would also like to thank Dr. Robert Knight, who helps train this process out in the field and works with schools and coaches to implement The Rhythm of the Learner Year in real-world settings.

We would also like to thank Iam Bennett for lending his artistic talents to the cover design and interior graphics, to Courtney Hudson and Camron Turner for their outstanding work on final design elements and typesetting, and to Kate Colbert and Penny Tate at Silver Tree Publishing for seeing the value in this idea and for bringing *Embracing the Rhythm of the Learner Year* to market.

While we cannot list them all by name, we would like to thank
the entire Ed Directions team — our leadership coaches, content
coaches, data coaches, project managers, administrators, marketers,
and support staff to whom this book is dedicated. They all played
a part in making this book and our methodology a success. This book
is the product of the important work they do every day.

GO BEYOND THE BOOK
AND KEEP IN TOUCH WITH EDUCATIONAL DIRECTIONS

The *Turning Around Turnaround Schools* book series, of which *Embracing the Rhythm of the Learner Year* is Volume 2, is just one of the many ways in which Frank DeSensi, Joe DeSensi, and the Educational Directions team serve America's K-12 educators.

Educational Directions specializes in customized academic improvement programs and strategies geared toward enhancing student performance, boosting leadership capabilities of school faculty and staff, and positively impacting the culture and outcomes of K-12 schools.

The experienced, passionate team at Educational Directions works with state, district, and school leaders to develop impact strategies that focus on three core change agents —creating a culture of learning, refocus planning around the student, and developing independent learners and performers (that, as a side benefit, become great test takers). Each track can then be aligned to specific grade levels, state standards, content areas, and individual school-specific needs.

Start a Conversation Today and Learn More About:

- Highly customized school turnaround programs

- Academic (district and school) leadership programs

- Professional development services for administrators and teachers

- Curricula development and curricula audits

- Climate audits and academic reviews

- And more ...

502-373-2700 | Info@EdDirections.com | EdDirections.com

ABOUT THE AUTHORS

FRANK DESENSI

Frank DeSensi is the founder and Chief Innovation Officer of Educational Directions, LLC, which consults with schools and school districts in the southeastern and midwestern United States. A retired educator, Frank spent 35 years in a variety of teaching and administrative positions. He taught at  the university, college, secondary, and middle-school levels; worked in the central office as a curriculum specialist; and held both principal and assistant principal positions. From 1993 to 1998, Frank served as a Kentucky Distinguished Educator, helping to turn around schools that were labeled in decline or in crisis under the provisions of the Kentucky Education Reform Act. Frank helped develop the STAR training program for new DEs and served as a trainer in the Kentucky Leadership Academy. He jointly holds patents for three data-management systems for schools.

JOE DESENSI, EdD

Joe DeSensi is the president of
Educational Directions, LLC. He has an
undergraduate degree from Bellarmine
University, a graduate degree in
computer-resource management from
Webster University, and a doctorate in
leadership education from Spalding
University. Dr. DeSensi has worked

with Fortune 500 companies, federal and local government, and
school districts across the Southeast and Midwest. He developed
custom and enterprise software to help districts track data and target
students' needs, and he holds patents in school data-management
software and database integration. Dr. DeSensi also teaches graduate classes in leadership, ethics, and strategic planning at Spalding
University.

Together Frank and Joe have authored two books in the *Turning
Around Turnaround Schools* series.

MISSED THE 1ST BOOK IN THE TURNING AROUND TURNAROUND SCHOOLS SERIES?

Before there was *Embracing the Rhythm of the Learner Year*, there was *What to Do When Conventional Wisdom and Best Practice Aren't Enough* ... the first Educational Directions book on turnaround work, which continues to serve as a practical guidebook for K-12 schools in an era of high-stakes accountability.

In a practical "what to do" format, Book #1 in the *Turning Around Turnaround Schools* series helps schools find targeted interventions for improving student achievement.

Available on Amazon in paperback and Kindle editions.

Made in the USA
Monee, IL
24 April 2020